D0403065

The Humanist Alternative:
some definitions of Humanism

The Humanist
Alternative:

some definitions of Humanism

edited by Paul Kurtz

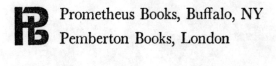

Prometheus Books, Buffalo, NY
Pemberton Books, London

First published 1973 by **Prometheus Books**,
923 Kensington Avenue, Buffalo, NY 14215
and Pemberton Books
London N1 8EN

SBN (US & Canada) 0 87975 013 8 *hardback*
0 87975 018 9 *paperback*

Printed in the United States of America

Preface:

The Meaning of Humanism

THE PRESENT CENTURY has been proclaimed as the Humanist century—the century in which anti-Humanist illusions inherited from previous ages have been seriously questioned and shattered. Humanism has historic roots in human civilization; yet it is only in recent times that these have begun to bear fruit. Using the powerful critical tools of science and logical analysis, modern man now recognizes that the universe has no special human meaning or purpose and that man is not a special product of creation. Anthropocentrism has at last been laid to rest. Modern man now realizes that he is responsible in large measure for his own destiny. Living on a minor planet on the edge of a small galaxy in a vast universe, man has come to see that he cannot look outside himself for salvation. His future, if he has any, is within his control.

But events are moving so rapidly that what is now at stake is the very survival of the human species itself. Science has emancipated man from the bondage of dogmatic religious mythology and it has provided him with the instruments for remaking and reordering his life, improving and enhancing it immeasurably. But whether he will be able to create a new and better world with vision and daring, or will destroy himself in the process is the real option that he now faces. The Humanist alternative offers him a realistic appraisal of the human condition and the promise of ameliorating it.

Many men and movements today profess to be Humanist. They recognize that what is at stake may be the continuance of the species man and that the population explosion, ecological pollution and nuclear warfare all threaten it. Thus a Humanist party has emerged to which all vow allegiance. But what is Humanism? What are its

5

ideals? What is its platform and programme? Is it primarily a religious doctrine, a scientific theory or an ethical code? It is apparent that there is considerable confusion about what the term Humanism implies. Indeed, there seem to be as many different varieties of Humanism as there are grades of wine and cheese. Is there a common theme underlying the Humanist message?

The term Humanism has been used in many senses. There are scientific, religious, atheistic and ethical Humanists. Indeed, many Marxists, existentialists, liberals, naturalists, experimentalists—even Christians—today claim to be Humanists. All loudly declare that they are *for man*, that they wish to actualize human potentialities, enhance human experience and contribute to happiness, social justice, democracy and a peaceful world. All say that they are opposed to authoritarian or totalitarian forces that dehumanize man. All profess compassion for human suffering and commitment to the unity of mankind.

Humanism thus provides a critique of alienating and depersonalizing tendencies, whether the source is religion, ideology, bureaucracy or technology. But does it have a positive message? Can it contribute to man's moral and ethical uplift? Can it provide meaning and direction for the good life? Or is the term 'Humanism', like the terms 'good', 'justice', 'beauty' and 'virtue', simply emotive, professed by men, yet without clear meaning? Is the word 'Humanist' to suffer the fate of the word 'Christian', that is, to become simply synonymous with an altruistic and humanitarian concern?

This symposium was initiated with these problems in mind. The contributors were asked the following questions:

> The term 'Humanism' is widely used, as are the terms 'ethical' Humanism, 'scientific' Humanism and 'religious' Humanism. What is Humanism? Can you define it? If there is in your judgment no clear definition in the literature, you may wish to propose one. You may also wish to focus on the relationship of Humanism to atheism, science, its ethical position, or some other theme.

Those who have contributed to this volume represent a wide spectrum of Humanist opinion in the world today. They are primarily philosophers, psychologists, social scientists, ethical and religious leaders. Among the themes they discuss are historic roots of Humanism, the general problem of definition, the relationship of Humanism to ethics and morality, Humanism and religion,

Humanism and atheism and Humanism on the world scene. Most of the varieties of Humanism are represented, including naturalistic Humanism, liberal Humanism, atheistic Humanism, humanistic psychology, behaviourism, Marxism and Zen. Virtually all the selections in this book were written especially for it, although a few have since been published in humanistic journals.

Given the wide diversity of Humanist viewpoints expressed in this volume, it should be clear that Humanism is not a dogma or creed. Although Humanists share a general point of view about man and his place in the universe; are critical of supernaturalistic religion or ideological dogma; and have a similar moral commitment to free thought, to the fulfilment of human potentialities and the democratic ideal of humanity as a whole, they nevertheless represent a wide range of opinion.

If there is a common thread running throughout this volume, it is the conviction that Humanism is committed to the method of reason as the chief means of solving problems and the belief that mankind can survive and humans can enjoy a significant life. This conviction and this belief, however, can be realized only if men continue to have confidence in their own natural powers and abilities and the courage to use them.

ACKNOWLEDGEMENTS

Some of the articles in this book, although written especially for it, have appeared in *The Humanist* magazine, and are reprinted by permission.

The epilogue, 'Is Everyone a Humanist?' by Paul Kurtz, originally appeared as 'The Humanist Ideal' in *Question 5* (1972).

Contents

I HISTORICAL ROOTS

I
Humanism's
Many Dimensions
EDWIN H. WILSON

THERE HAVE BEEN many Humanisms and their special emphases have each been designated by an endless array of adjectives. Christian Humanism, Greek Humanism, ethical Humanism, scientific Humanism, religious Humanism, rationalist Humanism and Humanistic Judaism are only a few of the many designations, but they are today important ones. One thing can be said, I believe, of all Humanisms that are worthy of the name: their central concern is for man, his growth, fulfilment and creativity in the here and now. Each variety of Humanism can be understood in terms of its causal sources and present programme.

The Christian Humanism that was nurtured in the Middle Ages by liberal bishops helped bring the Humanism of the Greeks down to the modern periods by means of the good libraries established by those bishops. That Christian Humanism was not anti-God but pro-man; it did not deny 'life eternal', but was concerned primarily with *this* life. Today various Christian scholars and Pope Paul are asserting that Humanism without God is futile. At the same time the liberals among the Christians are trying to recapture the word Humanism and make church ritual and actions more relevant to human need. If the action is the message—in part—there is much latent Humanism in both Jewish and Christian circles.

Religious Humanism, a term used in *A Humanist Manifesto* of 1933,[1] was based on the assumption that Humanism in a naturalistic frame is validly a religion; that all religions have been the pursuit of the ideal or the quest for the good life. The religions—natural and supernatural—are the efforts of men to be better than they are. They variously involve faith, aspiration, commitment, loyalty, hope and, sometimes, love.

[1] Sellars, Roy Wood (1933), 'A Humanist Manifesto' in *The New Humanist*, **VI**, 3.

The American Humanist Association (AHA) stemmed largely from Unitarianism as a movement of religious Humanists; but some Universalist ministers, Ethical Society leaders, scientists and philosophers also belonged. The writings of such pioneers as A. Eustace Haydon, Roy Wood Sellars, M. C. Otto, Sidney Hook, J. A. C. F. Auer and Corliss Lamont contributed depth and endurance to the movement.

Ethical Humanism grew principally out of the work of the American Ethical Union (AEU) and its emphasis on right relations between people as the most important thing. The ethical movement also considered itself religious and grew out of a religious background, but gradually moved from its earlier basis in Felix Adler's idealism toward a naturalistic frame with general acceptance of the scientific world view. Today the word Humanism has apparently gained equal status with the word Ethical in AEU. When Humanism was organized internationally in Amsterdam in 1952, its organization was called the International Humanist and Ethical Union (IHEU) to keep the ethical emphasis in the picture. Moreover, the Dutch Humanists, while disliking the adjective 'religious', were sceptical of science and regarded it more as a potential destroyer than as a 'saviour'. They were oriented toward social service, so the term Ethical seemed to be as appropriate as the term Humanist for them.

All the member organizations in the IHEU thus take on colouring and concerns that stem from their several histories and dominant personalities. In Norway and Germany, for instance, the Humanist associations accept subsidies from the state. In effect, they fill the place of a 'fourth faith', although the Norwegian Humanists do not call their organization religious. The Dutch Humanists press for recognition on a par with Catholics and Protestants, as in the furnishing of Humanist chaplains or counsellors in military, correctional and other state institutions. Human service is their thing. The Dutch movement had a fortunate founder in Professor Polak-Schwartz and also an equally able and versatile leader in Dr J. P. van Praag. The Canadian Humanist Association, the Radical Humanist Movement, the Norwegian Humanists (Humen-Etisk Forbund Norge) and, to an extent, the Korean Humanist Association, reflect the pressures of nationalism rather than basic ideological differences with the Humanism expressed in other places. The Humanist Union in India, by contrast, developed from a Rationalist

16

trend and is organized separately from the Radical Humanist Movement. At least thirty-three different Humanist associations in twenty-three countries are now enrolled in the International Humanist and Ethical Union.

Scientific Humanism arose through the thinking of John Dewey, Julian Huxley and others, but can be traced to Bacon's *Novum Organum.* ('Pursue science in order that the human estate may be enhanced.') Unlike some others, Dewey and Huxley affirmed religious Humanism, that is, religion without revelation. In the early 1940s, the Conference on the Scientific Spirit and Democratic Faith was formed. This brought the religious and ethical Humanists together with various other philosophers and scientists. Among those scientists were Dr Henry Margenau, Dr Gerald Wendt (later Editor of *The Humanist*), and Sir Richard Gregory. *The Humanist* magazine initiated a column called 'Science for Humanity', written by Dr Maurice Visscher. Physiologist A. J. Carlson was an early contributor. Dr Hermann J. Muller, a geneticist and Nobel Prize winner, served actively as President of the AHA for four years. Under Dr Muller, the AHA tended to become an organization of scientific Humanists, although educators such as W. H. Kilpatrick and George Axtelle also contributed importantly in work to maintain separation of Church and state. The religious emphasis in AHA gradually diminished to the point of dropping the word religion from the bylaws. It was, however, later restored.

The humanistic psychologists, with an organization of their own, remain officially isolated from other Humanist organizations but represent a blending of psychological science and ethical Humanism.

There were Humanists among both the conservative and reformed rabbis. Although staying close to liturgical forms of Judaism, the reconstructionist movement under Mordecai Kaplan was definitely Humanistic and naturalistic in its orientation. The work of Rabbi Sherwin T. Wine, who calls himself an 'ignostic', brought full acceptance of a scientific outlook and a naturalistic point of view. Rabbi Wine has organized the Society for Humanistic Judaism, a relatively recent organization, which aims to serve those people who identify themselves as Jewish by culture but reject theistic religion.

Another expression of Humanism in America has stemmed from the several Rationalist groups with successive organizations, largely the expression of individual leadership. Such 'free thought' Humanisms might be called rationalist Humanisms or secular Humanisms. A common error of such Humanists, particularly at the start, has been to identify Humanism too narrowly with negation of the supernatural and of immortality. All naturalistic Humanisms are secular in the sense of not being *under* God, but the rationalist, free thought, or secular Humanisms we designate here are anti-religious and anti-church. This negativism changes in particular individuals as the human usefulness and service orientation of an ethical society or liberal church fellowship manifest themselves in educational, psychological, humanitarian and activist dimensions. Humanism is always more than negative; it is essentially affirmative. The popular notion that religion is identically and exclusively concerned with God, immortality and revelation is denied in the writings of Curtis Reese, J. A. C. F. Auer, E. S. Ames, H. N. Wieman, Alfred Loisy, Julian Huxley, A. E. Haydon and many others. Humanism always includes a positive affirmation of values.

In Great Britain, the ethical societies and the Rationalist Press Association brought the ethical, rationalist and scientific factors in Humanism together in a high-level development guided by outstanding intellectual leaders and expanded slowly by persistent scientific and ethical publishing. The British Unitarian churches, tinged with the mysticism of Martineau and influenced by the omnipresent Church of England, cherished theistic respectability and, in the main, left the field wide open for the secular Humanist development by remaining predominantly worshipful, Bible-centred and 'Christian'. Hence organized Churches in Great Britain seldom give expression to naturalistic Humanism, whereas the British Humanists stress the secular and ethical side of Humanism. In Ireland, by contrast, the new Humanists, in a publication called *Nexus*, focus their attention on religion.

Broadly viewed, Humanism is a cultural movement with meanings and outcroppings not entirely expressed by the adjectives that have been applied to it, or that reflect it. It is broader than any of the organizations that attempt to represent it. Humanism courses through many institutions—religious, professional and cultural. It permeates society as a cultural happening wherever there are readers or thinkers. It is present in many activist thrusts, without conscious formulation. It centres in the faith that man can live a good life this side of the grave. It expresses the belief that man has potentially the intelligence, good will and co-operative skills to survive on this

18

planet, to explore space and to provide security and an opportunity for growth, adventure, meaning and fulfilment for all men. It is the faith that, however short may be man's days, beauty and joy may fill them.

2
Our Freethought Heritage:
The Humanist and
Ethical Movement
DAVID TRIBE

HERE IS A CLOSE PARALLEL between the history of ideas, the
history of words and the history of organizations. Words have
a catalytic effect on the mind and help to mould inchoate
ideas. Sometimes a number of words create essentially the same
idea from different angles. A new word, or an old word freshly
defined, may slightly refashion an old idea. When an idea is
sufficiently established, an organization is formed, taking as a name
the word in greatest vogue, upgrading it outliving it or abandoning,
it for another, according to relative dynamism.

A word that in many countries today comes to mind to describe
living without God is 'Humanism'. For many centuries it had no
necessary connotation of religious unbelief. It was a scholarly name
for certain literary and linguistic studies arising from the Renaissance, but as these led back to a Greco-Roman world whose
interest was in the human body, the interplay of human institutions,
rival religions and philosophies that stimulated the human mind,
and art as an expression of human creativity rather than as an
ancillary to devotions, there was in it the seeds of breakdown of the
medieval world view. The explicit rejection of religious dogmas had
been a tiny minority view from earliest times, but it grew into a
significant movement in the Christian world in eighteenth century
France. Here for the first and almost the only time, it mushroomed
into political power with the French Revolution. But revolutionary
emotions and institutions are both unstable, and political excesses
followed by counter-revolution discredited Age-of-Reason intellectuals abroad at the same time as they restored conservative society to
France. Nevertheless it was the influence of a Frenchman, Auguste

20

Comte, and his 'religion of humanity' that lent Humanism its non- or anti-Christian flavour. But those rituals and absolutes with which Comtism was associated were rather different from modern Humanism, which, although it had existed as a casual word from the second half of the nineteenth century, gained coherence only with the foundation of Humanist associations such as the American and the British Humanist Associations.

When I started writing the history of this world movement, with special emphasis on Britain, I chose a phrase that has had a longer consistent application: free thought. This was first assumed as a party label, in preference to 'atheism', by opponents of Christianity in sixteenth century France and Italy. When the word spread to England in the following century, it became associated with Herbert of Cherbury's 'deism', one of the many Anglo-Saxon compromises that have enabled people to ignore God without repudiating Him. This was closely analogous to modern unitarianism as elaborated in America, notably by Channing, in 1825.

Before the founding in 1866 in Great Britain of the National Secular Society, questioning of traditional values, political or ideological, had been largely a hobby for intellectuals. A few courageous writers, printers, agitators and politicians had sought to popularize these views and sometimes managed to form societies where the messages of great radicals like Thomas Paine were kept alive. But they were isolated enough for their groups to be declared illegal and for them to be picked off one by one. The bulk of the population consisted of either a conservative peasantry or a demoralized proletariat doing menial jobs in factories and mines, who were yet to gain industrial or political solidarity. Then the technological revolution accelerated, creating a demand for better-educated artisans. With education came political awareness, union organization, demands for suffrage and a challenge of those vested interests that opposed progress. It was soon seen that the Churches, with few exceptions, represented the *status quo* in all its aspects. But, as distinct from most political institutions, they had an intellectual and emotional hold on large sections of the population. Paine recognized that without an Age of Reason few people could see the Rights of Man. The emancipation of men's minds from ancient taboos, superstitions and dogmas, which had previously been deemed a largely upper-class pursuit of purely academic interest, was now seen to have political and social consequences. Free thinkers were

21

prepared to reveal themselves in sufficient numbers to make national movements possible and suppressions—as distinct from persecutions —impossible.

The words 'free' and 'thought' tell us much that is often forgotten by enemies and even by friends. Both are common words, the stock-in-trade of pedagogues and politicians alike. But they, or rather the ideas behind them, are not truly popular. Most people are afraid of freedom and thinking for themselves in the sense that their pater-nalistic authorities must be replaced by personal responsibility. The crowd mentality has flourished equally well in both the tribal and the urban jungles. What may be called the decline, if not the collapse, of traditional religious attitudes has not seriously eroded Church membership in America; and in Britain, where it has, it has not provided the market for Humanist recruitment that opti-mists had forecasted. Conversely, those who recognize that free thinkers are likely to be a perpetual minority, the flux in society's melting pot, often err in looking for them in one particular sector— a class, IQ range or professional spectrum. The combination of suitable affective and intellectual qualities is not necessarily to be found in intellectuals, and formal education can be a conformist rather than a liberating process. Generally speaking, however, the lowest strata of society have not been reached (any more than by the Churches) and adherents have tended to have a personal drive and sparkle, an ambition for their children if not for themselves, that have competed favourably with more mercenary groups. Their social rise from the nineteenth into the twentieth century has more than matched the general *embourgeoisement* of the community.

Whereas in other groups this rise has usually been accompanied by a suburban political shift to the Right, the freethought movement has tended to stay radical, wishing to see the gulf between the haves and the have-nots narrow. This is particularly true in Europe, where the Roman Catholic Church more overtly interferes in politics on the side of the ruling classes, and radical opposition springs naturally from the churchless. In the Anglo-Saxon world it is a mistake, especially in the disintegrating political life of our times, to say simply that a Humanist is a man of the Left, as A. J. Ayer has done. A hundred years ago in Britain he was almost certain to be in the Liberal party; and in the United States, with its then dominant English traditions and the universal free thought opposition to slavery, he was in the Republican party. The political complexion and fortunes of these parties have since changed and Left-wingers as such have generally moved over to British *New Statesman/Tribune* Labour or New Deal 'dove' Democrats. But this is by no means universal for free thinkers, whose suspicion of slogans and panaceas has filtered their progressivist vision. What is characteristic is their utilitarian conception—the greatest happiness of the greatest number, in which they see both material and spiritual aspirations—which has kept them away from political extremism of the far Right or far Left, in whose name personal liberty is usually sacrificed to an abstract ideal.

Free thought implies philosophical interest. At first sight it might imply philosophical nihilism. But human psychology shows that permanent suspension of opinion is neurosis and not enlightenment. Free thinkers do come to specific views which, though neither absolute nor rigid, are implied in the names of their organizations: secular, ethical, rationalist, progressive, personalist, humanist. Interestingly, these names are not philosophical terms, nor are they used in the technical sense of philosophers. Some of the earliest freethought societies were called eclectic, to emphasize this independence of philosophical schools. But certain orientations have been more common than others. Though famous Humanists like Corliss Lamont champion philosophical naturalism, most have been materialists and determinists.

Just as they give no automatic allegiance to any system of thought, so do they not accept theories of science, politics or sociology simply on the basis of current popularity. Dogmas may flourish in the university no less than in the temple. One thinks of Piltdown man, Lysenko biology, faculty flirting with mediumship and parapsychology, scientology, phrenology and extreme claims for mesmerism or hypnotism. The most influential and obvious political myths have flourished under the banner of communism, but they are not unknown in liberal democracy—the British rule of law, the American way of life—and nineteenth century free thinkers themselves tended to succumb to the prevailing liberal cult of inevitable progress. It is important to emphasize these concerns, for the most characteristic, and hence most cited, feature of free thought is its opposition to religion or at least to organized dogmatic religion. The British South Place Ethical Society is still dedicated to the 'cultivation of a rational religious sentiment'. And it is often common for certain segments of the ethical movement in America, the home

23

of Felix Adler's Ethical Culture in 1876, to consider itself a manifestation of naturalistic religion—although the American Ethical Union is now thoroughly humanistic in outlook. The newly-founded Fellowship of Religious Humanists in the United States also focuses on the religious aspects of Humanism. Secularism, which originated from the 'rational religion' of Owenism as well as from the political radicalism of Chartism, similarly had in its early days secular hymns and Sunday schools, ritual anniversaries and name-giving ceremonies. These features have long since disappeared from all secular societies, and have never been a part of the newer Humanist groups; but a few leading figures like Julian Huxley still suggest that Humanism is itself the basis of a new religion.

Many Humanists have disputed this, pointing out that the traditional accoutrements of religion clinging in threadbare tatters even to modernist churches—creeds, sacraments, scriptures, consecrated ministers, to say nothing of gods, for what they may be worth in a modern world—have been shed by the Humanist movement. Up until a few years ago it could be said that the most significant characteristic of free thought was atheism or a milder substitute like agnosticism, scepticism or nontheism. This has recently been upset by the 'Death of God' school of Christian atheism. But with some justification, Marxists and *Brave New World* scientists see the Western Humanist movement as in the religious tradition, not because its answers to human problems are the same, but because it is concerned with the same questions and has something of the same emotional dynamic. Credence is given to this view because some of the most brilliant Humanist organizers and propagandists, people like Charles Bradlaugh, John and Charles Watts, G. J. Holyoake, Annie Besant, Moncure Conway, F. J. Gould, Robert Ingersoll and Joseph McCabe had originally been clerics, related to clerics or strongly influenced by religion in early life. Many of them were prosecuted, imprisoned or otherwise persecuted for their beliefs, as the Christian martyrs had been.

The free thinkers themselves have dismissed this connection, insisting that they repudiated their past in every way, that their world view became naturalistic instead of super-naturalistic, and that this brought about an utterly changed conception of man, the universe and his place in it. This is best seen in a historical context. On many social questions today there seems to the outsider little difference between the views of Humanists and those of liberal religionists. Perhaps the chief aspect of the free-thought movement is that its growth has not been so much by direct proselytizing as by ideological osmosis. The influence of free thinkers is not to be seen in the numbers that have joined their organizations or stood up on the fringe to be counted or in the popularity that atheism enjoys in the world at large. It is in the way that people's vital secondary beliefs have been affected, whatever their views on ultimate reality, whether they stay inside or leave the Churches. It is seen in their generally more critical assessments of scriptures and sacraments, in the dwindling conviction that unbelievers will be universally damned and in the rapid extinguishing of hellfire. And it is seen in their social attitudes and in their view of man as having a self-made destiny and one world to achieve it in. This concept alters our whole approach to society. Present injustices cannot be related to a divine plan, or future hopes to a heavenly consummation. It is a mistake to say that Humanists are obsessed with the 'negative' task of demolishing religion or with rarefied intellectual problems of interest to no one but themselves. It is here and now that wrongs must be righted.

Some short-term goals can be achieved by political organization: abolition of slavery, universal suffrage, trade unionism, social security, protection of tenants and graduated taxation. Others are longer educative processes: the equality of women, the rights of children and animals, international arbitration instead of war, world government, population control, conservation, law reform and racial integration. Before popular education was established or generally regarded as desirable, free thinkers were calling for free, secular and compulsory education. They saw it as more than just a meal ticket in a scientific age. It was a way to reshape fundamental human attitudes in the image of liberalism and understanding. In countries without a secular constitution (and even in the others, when vigilance is lacking) religion intrudes into the school day not only to seek converts but to suggest that ethics and social commitment ought to depend on religion. Not only is this a violation of academic and democratic principles, but it impairs the contribution education might make to morality and citizenship, to awareness of the common humanity of man. In the absence of state provision of suitable classes in ethics, the free-thought organizations of some countries provide them for at least their own members' children.

The philosophical materialism that is widespread among free thinkers has over the past century needed to distinguish itself from

25

dialectical materialism and popular materialism. Another confusion, genuine or contrived, derives from the assumption that those who follow science to the exclusion of religion in the physical and social spheres must be lacking in sensitivity and aesthetic appreciation, if not in moral awareness. It is, however, easy to show that many of the leading writers, musicians and artists of this, as of other periods, were, and are, convinced free thinkers. The not infrequent allegation that Humanists are immoral results from similar ignorance or malevolence and also from real controversy over definitions. To most Christians immorality is a sin that ought to be a crime. In theory it may include almost any act of commission or omission, but the New Testament and convention have combined to equate it with a sexual peccadillo. Humanists respond first of all by saying that this is too narrow and too trivial an assessment. There are more important ethical concerns than sexual lapses: cruelty, greed, intolerance, slander, untrustworthiness. Nor do Humanists necessarily accept the culpability pronouncements of Christians in sexual fields.

People are infinitely varied in their natures and their needs. Desires cannot automatically be accepted and satisfied, and education aims at fostering discrimination and self-control. But insofar as this simply reduces the individual's happiness without advancing that of others, it is not virtue but masochism. Much irregular sexuality and 'obscene' literature come into this consideration. Some people are heterosexual, some homosexual. So long as harmful social consequences, notably venereal disease and unwanted children, are avoided and personal integrity and respect for others is sustained, it is of little ethical consequence what an individual's sexual behaviour might be. Stable unions seem to be in the best interests of offspring, but if a mistake is made and dependents are looked after, divorce should be readily available. In any case illegitimate children should not suffer for their parents' actions. Euthanasia, abortion, family planning and suicide are other matters that should be left to the individual conscience. There are admittedly anti-social acts that have to be legislated against, but the important thing in penology is to understand why a criminal has taken to crime and to seek to reform him. In all these fields, notably in contraception and abortion-law reform, free thinkers have played a dominant, almost a unique role.

Freedom is concerned with areas other than permissiveness in sexual and family legislation and the basic provisions of political democracy. It is concerned with the implementation of a secular or open society, where individuals are free to express their views with minimal hindrance, in the public interest, publicly or privately, in limited or in mass circulation media. No privileges based on politics or religion, no religious tests in the professional or social lives of citizens, no established Churches, no universal keeping of holy days, no violent conflict on the basis of birth or credal differences. These are aspirations of free thinkers throughout the world. Labels within the movement vary in place and time, but the torch that has been handed down from generation to generation, from country to country, shines the same bright rays in the same dark corners.

II GENERAL PROBLEMS
OF DEFINITION

3
The Snare
of Definitions

SIDNEY HOOK

HE LOGIC OF DEFINITIONS is quite complex. Unless we are clear about the point and purpose of a definition, its context in use and inquiry, it may create more difficulties than it solves.

This is particularly true with respect to the definition of Humanism. One danger lies in defining Humanism so broadly that it includes many who have defended monstrous crimes against human freedom; who have, for instance, been professional apologists of Stalin's terroristic regime, including the infamous Moscow Purge Trials and other practices exposed by Khruschev in his Report to the Twentieth Congress of the CPSU. Some definitions of Humanism are so broad that they would embrace defenders of the regimes of Salazar and Franco, who also profess a belief in 'the brotherhood of man'. Such definitions of Humanism are as worthless as definitions of 'democracy' (very fashionable these days) that include perfervid partisans of minority party dictatorships.

The converse difficulty is defining Humanism too narrowly. We then exclude individuals with whom we feel a strong moral kinship and who, despite some metaphysical or even theological overbeliefs that seem to have no perceptible bearing on their conduct, are comrades, or at least co-belligerents, in every good cause. Any definition that excludes them seems inadequate.

This was brought home to me by a remark of John Dewey many years ago. During the 1930s some Jewish rabbis were great admirers of the Soviet Union and were, in effect, Stalinist fellow-travellers on the ground, among other reasons, that there was no official anti-Semitism in communist Russia. To be sure, Stalin was depriving many Jews of their freedom and sometimes of their lives but not *as* Jews, merely as human beings no different from Ukrainians,

31

Russians, Americans and even Georgians who disagreed or were suspected of disagreeing with him. Since Jews were being treated or mistreated equally, they contended that this was preferable to the overt and covert anti-Semitism in Czarist Russia, Western Europe and the United States. At the suggestion of Henry Hurwitz, the editor of *The Menorah Journal*, I wrote an article entitled 'Promise Without Dogma: A Social Philosophy for Jews'. In it I argued that any member of the Jewish minority who was concerned with the survival of Jewish culture or religion should resolutely defend a social philosophy committed to five cardinal principles: (1) cultural pluralism; (2) religious tolerance and independence of Church and state; (3) political democracy; (4) democratic socialism, if this was the only way poverty could be abolished and a genuine welfare state established; and (5) the centrality of intelligence, the paradigm of which was the *pattern* of scientific inquiry as the method of resolving social conflicts.

Dewey had received a copy of the magazine. When next we met, he said: 'That was an excellent article, Sidney'. He then added with a twinkle in his eye, 'What I don't understand is why you left me out. I believe all that—and have for a long time. Does that make me an honorary Jew?'

Formally, of course, there was nothing wrong in recommending something to Jews that was universally valid. What was good for everybody was good for the Jews too! But I felt rather foolish since I knew that I would never have written a piece on 'Arithmetic for the Jews' in order to tell them that $2+2=4$, or on 'Health for the Jews' stressing the universal principles of hygiene like exercise and a balanced diet. I tried to explain to Dewey that it was really written for the benefit of fellow-travelling rabbis—a species of hypocritical gentry who still exist today. No longer able to extenuate the Kremlin's cultural and religious oppression of Jewry, they now draw equations between the domestic and foreign policies of the United States and those of Nazi Germany and Stalin's Russia.

Definitions of Humanism should avoid the pitfall of so defining it that it excludes no one. If the Holy Grail is everywhere there is no point in its quest! For example, in an otherwise historically scholarly article in the *Encyclopaedia of Philosophy*[1] we are told that: 'Humanism is also any philosophy which recognizes the value or dignity of man and makes him the measure of all things or somehow [*sic!*]

[1] Edwards, Paul (ed) (1967), *Encyclopaedia of Philosophy*, New York: Macmillan

takes human nature, its limits, or its interests as its theme.' Surely this is too broad! It catches almost everyone in its far-flung net. Who denies the value of man? Not even the Torquemadas of this world. Since *both* Protagoras and Socrates are Humanists, it is not necessary to make the view that man is the measure of all things a necessary element in the definition of Humanism. It would exclude not only Socrates but atheistic Humanists like Bertrand Russell and Morris R. Cohen to whom the Protagorean dictum was anathema. To them, the proposition that man is the measure of all things is an expression of self-defeating subjectivity.

As a first step towards clarification of issues and standpoints, I should like to propose that Humanism today be regarded primarily as an *ethical* doctrine and movement. We already have a term in use, the connotations of which embrace what is generally meant by 'scientific Humanism'—viz. 'naturalism'.

There are Humanists who are naturalists (John Dewey), Humanists who are supernaturalists (like William James) and Humanists who are non-naturalists (like Felix Adler and G. E. Moore). These men differ not in their chief ethical values but in their meta-ethical analysis of the meanings and justification of the 'good' and 'right'.

Religion, as a system of overbeliefs about the existence of God and related views, I regard as a *private* matter. So long as I am not requested to give it any public support or affirmation, I have no more desire to expose, refute or confound it than I do my neighbour's belief that his wife is the most beautiful woman in the world. (The 'truth' is, of course, that mine is!) I have grown weary of being told that my 'concern' with human freedom or the 'fire in my heart' that blazes up when I hear of human cruelty is evidence of my religious nature.

Abstractly, except when two terms are exhaustive and exclusive of the alternatives, it is absurd to define a term by its negations, for such definition does not distinguish it from other terms in an indeterminedly large universe of discourse. But in specific, historical contexts sometimes we can make progress towards an adequate definition when we stress what we want to exclude.

I do not regard as Humanists today any individuals or groups:

(1) who believe or support doctrines and practices that would impose one pattern of culture, language and life-style on all members or groups in the community;

B

(2) who believe in an established Church or Churches, or that they have been vouchsafed revelations about their special character, justifying privileges and rights denied to other human beings;

(3) who believe in or support through their own voluntary activities dictatorships of minority political parties no matter whether they are called 'organic', 'directed', 'higher' or 'socialist' democracies;

(4) who deny community responsibility for the elimination of human hunger and for the progressive realization of civilized standards of housing, health, welfare and education;

(5) who denigrate the use of intelligence, justify violence in human affairs as the most effective method of achieving social reform, substitute lynch law (white or black) for judicial process, oppose *opportunities* for racial integration;

(6) who place loyalty to any organization of which they are members above any or all of the above values, who cherish any truth, offered as a ground for public action, above the evidence on which it allegedly rests, who profess to be tolerant but who, out of stupidity or cowardice, tolerate those who are actively intolerant in social and, especially, intellectual life.

If I had to propose a short positive definition on the basis of these negations, I would say that an ethical Humanist today is one who relies on the arts of intelligence to defend, enlarge and enhance the areas of human freedom in the world. Ethical Humanists may differ from each other, but they respect those with whom they disagree. They are not fanatics of virtue. They recognize that good conflicts with good, right with right, and sometimes the good with the right. To these conflicts they bring the only value that is also the judge of its own efficacy and limitation—human intelligence.

4
A Definition
of Humanism

H. J. BLACKHAM

I DEPRECATE ANY DEFINITION of Humanism that mutilates it
with an epithet—'ethical', 'scientific', 'religious'. For this gives
exclusive or special right to a selected aspect of human life
and maims the body of all-round Humanist concern with human
being. A unicorn is fascinating; but one averts the eyes from a
bird with one wing. Of course, in a special context it may be
appropriate to use an epithet; but that is application, not definition.

Humanism, then, is a concept of man. There are many such
concepts and men have not agreed about them, and are not likely
to for some time to come. I would distinguish between a concept
of human nature, which might be a synthesis of relevant knowledge
on which general agreement could be expected and worked for,
and concepts of man which go beyond information—as Humanism
does.

Many concepts of man have been therapeutic: man is sick, not
his true self, in the sense that he is 'fallen' (Christianity), 'earth-
bound' (Hinduism, Buddhism), 'empirically worthless' (Hegel),
'alienated' (Marxism), 'inauthentic' (existentialism). In each case
there is a justifying total view and a dependent strategy for living:
man becomes his true self by obedience to the divine will, by
conformity to the cosmic design, by identification with Being or
with historical process, by assuming his autonomy in the continuous
exercise of choice. Some of these concepts are historical, some
metaphysical; some are centred in the cosmos, some in the Creator,
some in man himself or in a transaction in which he is partner. All
have sophisticated traditions that make these abrupt references
look like lines of a caricature.

35

Humanism too has a long tradition. It is historical rather than metaphysical (and therefore Western rather than Eastern), and it is centred in man but is distinct in being neither therapeutic nor dualistic. It is less ready to differentiate between what man is and what he ought to be and refuses to define him in terms of a universal given end. This is by no means because of complacency about man and his future. Rather, it is because of a sensitive regard for each man as his own end and for man as responsible for man. This notion of human responsibility is the nuclear idea in the definition of Humanism. There is no entelechy, no built-in pattern of perfection. Man is his own rule and his own end. Human life is in human hands. The strategy for living is 'adopt and adapt', not 'obey' or 'conform'.

This view is both prescriptive and unprescriptive. It is prescriptive in being a concept of man and a strategy for living; unprescriptive in leaving ends open. As Nietzsche observed, if man is totally responsible and there is no built-in order, if ends are open and history is merely 'a great index of human possibilities', everything is permissible. Here Humanism is the human decision to give moral equivalence to all men as human beings. Acceptance of interdependence and the solidarity of interests as the basis of human relations means acceptance of a share in joint responsibility for creating for all the conditions of a life worthy to be called human, a human providence in which each may be his own end without mockery.

Thus Humanism calls man to a human programme. The main features of this programme are familiar: international security, aid, conservation, population control, development and direction of technology, education for autonomy and an open society. Such a formidable global programme is liable to leave the ordinary Humanist, who is trying to make a living, slightly defeatist or cynical. Here is Humanist faith, a reasonable faith in intelligent action. The character of the programme is such that its call comes home to everyone's possibilities to respond.

On the basis of this interdependence, there remains the inalienable responsibility of each for himself as his own end. It is the glory of Humanism that here it is unprescriptive but may be exemplary. Personal life is choice not obligation, a work of art not a set task, an offering not a requirement, a creation not a prize.

36

Abstractly, then, Humanism is a concept of man focused upon a programme for humanity. Concretely, it is my idea of, and my commitment to, my part in that programme, which includes not least the life that is in my own hands.

5
Toward a
Definition of Humanism
JOSEPH L. BLAU

ONSIDER, FOR A MOMENT, AN ACORN. We may say that it has a natural end: to become an oak tree. We may add that this natural end includes the perpetuation of its species. The acorn is not conscious of its end. We should not speak, for instance, of the end as purposed, nor of the acorn as motivated by self- or species-preservation. The realization of its end (its natural teleology, in Aristotelian terms) is an unfolding of latencies, not an ethical striving.

Again, consider a boar. Once more, we may say that it has an end: self-preservation, and thereby the perpetuation of its species. Realization of the natural end of the boar, however, may preclude realization of the natural end of the acorn. But the boar is conscious neither of its own end nor of how it frustrates the acorn's. The boar does not have a purpose that motivates it to eat acorns in order to prevent their developing into oak trees. The boar has instincts that impel it to eat acorns to fulfil its natural teleology. It does not consider its own welfare, still less the welfare of the acorn. A boar cannot be judged ethically.

Now let us turn to the human species. Man, too, has a natural end, even as has a boar or an acorn. In a sense, his natural end is as fundamentally decisive for him as is the natural end of an acorn or a boar. To the extent that this is so, that the human being is a creature of his nature, the human *telos* is self- and species-preservation. But members of the human race are conscious of their natural end and are, therefore, in a position to judge means as contributory or noncontributory to this end. The reservoir of means that have been judged contributory is the culture of humankind.

Human culture includes science (what humanity has found out about its surroundings) as well as ethics (what humanity has found out about its internal relations). Science, we say, is self-corrective; the continued application of those very techniques that have led to incorrect or inadequate judgments about human surroundings will lead to the correction and reformulation of these judgments. We do not recognize or sufficiently stress that ethics, too, is self-corrective. As time goes on, humankind has reformulated many erroneous earlier ethical judgments in accordance with the results of increased ethical awareness. These changes are slower than those resulting from the self-corrective method of science, and at some times in the history of mankind the chasm between human knowledge and its application to the ethical relations of persons and groups seems unbridgeable.

Human culture includes art (the concrete expression of human ideals in plastic forms) as well as ethics (the abstract expression of human ideals in the form of principles). In either form, the human activity of projecting ideals as goals is purposive. For the human species, ends are transformed into targets. This is not the case in the rest of the range of natural being, from acorn and boar to yak and zebra. Humankind transforms even its natural end into a purposed goal. It strives consciously toward the improvement of its own species, not merely toward its perpetuation. Individual members of the species, in seeking self-improvement, attempt to apply general ethical principles to the re-creation of themselves as works of art and thus the members can contribute purposively to the improvement of the human species.

The acorn in its unfolding cares not in the least whether boar or human survives or perishes. The boar in its blind lust for survival is unconcerned with the fate of human or acorn. Human purposes, however, can and often do include care and concern for oaks and boars insofar as the survival, and, indeed, the improvement, of oaks and boars contributes to the realization of human ends. Only recently have human science, art and ethics come to know how profoundly implicated in human welfare are oaks and boars and other natural beings, and we see already a shifting of human goals toward more pervasive ecological concern.

If, in the vagrant processes of nature, a thinking acorn were to come into being, its philosophy and its religion would be limited by its quercine nature. Its metaphysic would deal with reality from the perspective of the oak; it could not admit the reality of the boar (the boar would be 'no thing'). If the artful imaginings of George

39

Orwell's *Animal Farm*[1] were to occur in nature and thinking boars come into being, their philosophy and religion would be restricted by their nature's conceiving of all reality as relating to swine. (*Quercianism* and *suidianism* might be appropriate names for these processes.) For us, the case is different. 'Man,' said Diderot, 'is the single place from which we must begin and to which we must refer everything.' But, as we have seen, human reality includes oaks and boars as well as people. Human imagination can 'take the role of the other' even when that other is not human. Human good can include the good of oaks and swine. '*Homo sum*,' said Terence, 'I am a human being; I regard nothing of human concern as alien to me.'

This is Humanism, a philosophy as natural to humankind as quercianism to the acorn or suidianism to the boar. It is an ethical philosophy because it sets forth principled goals for self- and species-improvement. It is grounded in human culture, and therefore rests on both art and science. It is an inclusive philosophy, for better oaks and better swine are incorporated into its quest for the betterment of humankind.

[1] Orwell, George (1945), *Animal Farm*, London: Secker and Warburg

6

Humanist Responsibilities

HORACE L. FRIESS

THE CURRENT QUALIFICATIONS of Humanism as scientific, as ethical, as religious, properly represent compelling interests within the whole. Each interest is vital enough to merit emphasis, if this is coupled with due recognition of specific responsibilities. The particular charge of scientific Humanism is to give us our most reliable knowledge of how things happen in the continuity of man and nature. It is our strongest resource for effective operations. Its connection with naturalism bars an impoverishing concentration on man in isolation from the rest of the world. It also enforces the moral discipline of thorough inquiry and objective thinking.

Ethical Humanism has a focal interest for integrity and justice in the treatment of persons and groups. It is not wedded to a fixed moral code, but is concerned with the development of standards in these matters; in a world of suffering it would extend an ethic of compassion. It seeks constructive paths towards non-exploitive relations and toward freeing people for mutually supportive growth.

Religious Humanism primarily means a dedication to Humanist values and a nurturing of faith in them. It may also include an interest in worthy celebration of life's crises and triumphs. Beyond these points it has a tendency toward a cosmic range of feeling, appreciation and apprehension. It wants its sense of human greatness to be in keeping with a sense of 'other' greatness whether in nature or in imagined ideal realms. Such experience may be intensely mystical.

These several interests within Humanism can develop appropriate strengths with responsible regard for one another and for the whole. Or they can thwart one another by illusory estimates of their own competences. Some lively tension between them, and debate over limits, should be taken as a healthy sign of adventurous thought.

41

But aggrandizing claims to self-sufficiency on any side are unimpressive except as instances of fallible human zeal.

The unprecedented situation into which contemporary man has recently come has critical implications for Humanism. The growing world population, global communication, the powers of technology for despoliation and death as well as for better life are all conditions with a new impact. Novel co-operation on a world scale has become necessary for survival; generous freedom for variety remains necessary for an excellence of life worthy of man's potentialities.

Indeed, 'man is so fearfully and wonderfully made' as to revive a strong sense of paradox in the light of his condition today. A Thoreau withdrawing into remote places to hear the hermit thrush *may* be more of a Humanist than many who congest city traffic and rejoice in ever faster travel. The claim to a Humanist regard for today's counter-cultural revolt cannot be bypassed although it is coupled with much restive alienation or wanton destructiveness. A dynamic Humanism must afford room for transcendence of the existing cultural state.

In every culture, what is definitely Humanist is often alloyed with traits that are not normative for all Humanism. Humanism involves recognizing human dignity and power in some of its important dimensions, accepting responsibility for their cultivation and for making them effective in the whole sense of life. In general, we can define Humanism as a perceptive loyalty to man and a generous caring for him. Its universal tendency is to stress human self-understanding and self-determination.

To find nothing alien that is human should mean a willingness to wrestle critically, but as a comrade, with the presented human condition. What is anti-Humanist can also be identified in many aspects; it is familiar in blue-nosed misanthropy, in rude know-nothingism and in all-too-common ignorance and meanness. There is also much anti-Humanism in partisan *hubris* and in a general human arrogance or reckless defiance toward the nonhuman world. Contemporary Humanism faces a crisis brought on by Faustian man in his urge toward limitless transformations. Can we find proportion before we destroy ourselves through our own productiveness?

7
What is Humanism?

J. P. VAN PRAAG

IS IT POSSIBLE TO DEFINE the concept of Humanism? In my view
it is not possible in the sense in which scientific concepts are
defined. The latter are shaped for the purpose of serving in a
more theoretical framework of coherent notions. They can be
unambiguously defined by eliminating confusing existential
elements. Humanism, on the contrary, is what it is through its
existential value. It is bound up with emotions and evaluations.
It is a moral conviction rather than a theoretical speculation.
Therefore it is more suited for a clarifying description than for an
unambiguous definition.

Such a description should be both clear and broad. That is, it
should explain in its coherence as strictly as possible the differences
from other convictions, and it should as far as possible include all
varieties of Humanism, such as ethical, scientific, religious and
social varieties of the basic idea. This requires a description that is
limited to essentials and yet includes all the essentials of the various
types of Humanism, so that their adherents can recognize themselves
in the given description.

In principle there are, in my opinion, two approaches to a description of Humanism; namely, an approach from the point of view of
what it starts from and an approach from the point of view of what
it stands for. The first approach leads to a phenomenological
description and the second one to a statement of aims.

Is it possible to formulate the starting points that are basic for
all Humanists? To do so, one must try to discover in modern
Humanism the elements that precede any special interpretation of
it. These would describe the mental attitude that can be conceived
as the common denominator of the various forms of Humanism.

An attempt to formulate some of these starting points is provided
by the following set of postulates.

(1) Equality. Men are of a similar biological and mental structure. In view of this similarity the undeniable differences between men appear irrelevant. By this conception men live principally in a common world.

(2) Secularity. Men spring from a world of which they are a natural part. They form a unity of body and consciousness—they are junctions of relations. But they are also centres of action. As intentional beings they shape their world.

✗ (3) Liberty. As relatively indefinite beings, men must shape their lives by deciding in freedom. Freedom means freedom of choice (be it determined or not). By self-determination men give their lives human meaning.

(4) Fraternity. Men are designated for community; the community shapes the individual. Self-determination in community provides for both the meaning of human life and a standard for (moral) judgment.

(5) Evaluation. Men are evaluating beings. Reason is rationally applied to evaluations. It is the best of judgment and responsibility.

(6) Experience. The world can be experienced by identification and observation. Identification is synthetical and provides religious experience; observation is analytical and provides knowledge.

(7) Existence. World and men exist (are perceptible) in indissoluble coherence. Men and world are conceived as interdependent. The world is, in principle, a human world, and men are secular beings.

(8) Completeness. The world is complete. That does not mean that it is perfect, but that it is not thought of as dependent on a creator nor that there is an empty place left vacant by an absent creator.

(9) Evolution. The world is dynamic in its evolutionary and causal structure. It is conceived as developing in lawful coherence. This is the formula of its dynamic character and it enables men to live with reality and to act upon it.

Find own meaning (10) Contingency. The world does not by itself reveal meaning. Man can contribute meaning to his existence by his interpretation of reality.

This outline by no means represents the variety of Humanist conceptions. It simply aims at explaining the common basis of Humanist thinking and acting. The other approach would express the common aims of various types of Humanism. I would suggest here that they might be formulated as follows:

Humanism is a moral conviction characterized by the attempt to understand life and the world and to act in it by appealing exclusively to human faculties; and it is directed towards everyone's self-determination in a common humanity. It naturally considers all fixed positions as subject to discussion. However, it reminds us of certain ideas that under varying circumstances must be converted into concrete purposes. Some of its basic conceptions can serve not so much to explain Humanism as to clarify what it aims at.

(1) Humanism attempts to provide a coherent answer to the questions of human existence and assumes that existence can be made worthwhile by the realization of everyone's possibilities in devotion to a common humanity.

(2) It acknowledges the possibility of the experience of an inscrutable coherence and of a notion of promising development, but it requires also continuous readiness to reasonable and scientific justification of thought and action.

(3) Humanist morality is based on the acknowledgment of the mutual solidarity of men and their equivalence in the consideration of their interests and aspirations; it is directed towards the maturity of all men.

(4) Humanism demands from society that it creates conditions for the free development of individuals and groups in the form of prosperity, equity, legality, participation and self-government.

(5) It aims at an open society characterized by freedom of opinion, readiness to deliberate, mutual respect and democratic procedures, and directed towards the general welfare.

III MORALITY AND HUMANISM

8

Humanism and
the Moral Revolution

PAUL KURTZ

UMANISTS HAVE BEEN DEBATING for years the proper definition of Humanism. It is clear that Humanism is not a dogma or creed and that there are many varieties of, and meanings given to, Humanism. Nevertheless, one may suggest at least four characteristics that contemporary Humanists emphasize.

First, Humanists have some confidence in man and they believe that the only bases for morality are human experience and human needs. Second, many or most Humanists are opposed to all forms of supernaturalistic and authoritarian religion. Third, many Humanists believe that scientific intelligence and critical reason can assist in reconstructing our moral values. And fourth, Humanism is humanitarian in that it is concerned with the good life and social justice as moral ideals.

Humanism as a movement is wide enough to include many people who will agree with some of the above points, but not all. What characterizes an increasing number of people is a commitment to a moral point of view in which mankind is viewed as a whole. Such a characteristic does not make one a Humanist by itself. Yet, it is an ideal that most Humanists share. Humanists may honestly disagree about their political beliefs and about many social questions. There is no Humanist party line. What Humanists today share in common, however, are a concern for humanity, a belief that moral values must be removed from the mantle of theological dogma, and a conviction that our moral ideals must be constantly re-examined and revised in the light of present needs and social demands.

The present epoch is a revolutionary one, involving a radical questioning of basic foundations, structures, beliefs and values. In the present context Humanism has become especially identified with the moral revolution. It is this aspect that I wish to focus upon.

49

There have been many kinds of revolution in human history: political, economic, social, scientific. The revolution that we are experiencing today is a moral revolution. Although it has many dimensions, at its roots the revolution is humanistic. It involves a critique of religious, ideological and moralistic philosophies that tend to deny or denigrate the most genuine qualities of human existence. And it is an attempt to recover those human aspects of life that have been lost in post-industrial society.

The overthrow of customary morality has occurred in large part because of an explosive technology that has rapidly transformed our culture. A sharp disparity has emerged between the new technology and our inherited moral codes. The latter were encased in custom, enshrined in sacred tradition and supported by the sanction of law. The moral tradition was taken as absolute—unquestionable and beyond the range of critical inquiry. The strains between the received morality and the demands of modern life were too great; the moral 'virtues' were out of touch with the world and practice deviated widely from professed ideals.

Suddenly, the dam has burst and the old moral mythology is now being lampooned. There is a long-overdue demand for reappraisal and modification. A moral reconstruction is proceeding at an accelerated pace.

There are both negative and positive aspects to the current moral reformation. It involves a devastating critique of the hypocrisy and injustice of the Establishment, but it also involves a creative effort to develop new moral ideals more appropriate to the world in which we live. Several ideals are being proclaimed at the same time. These are often unclear and confused.

The basic assumption of the new morality is the conviction that the good life is achieved when we realize the human potential. This means that we ought to reject all those creeds and dogmas that impede human fulfilment or impose external authoritarian rules upon human beings. The traditional supernaturalistic moral commandments are especially repressive of our human needs. They are immoral insofar as they foster illusions about human destiny and suppress vital inclinations.

The moral revolution rejects those impersonal bureaucratic organizations that smother individuality and restrict human autonomy. The new morality is appreciative of the fact that modern technology has provided great benefits for the good life—that it has

50

helped to eliminate the scourges of disease, hunger, drudgery and misery. But the new morality is especially critical of the dehumanizing and depersonalizing aspects of technology. It attacks the fact that man increasingly tends to lose his sense of responsibility and his appetite for creativity in the highly complex society in which we now live. Human alienation is accentuated by the banality of a consumer-oriented, manipulative economic system that conditions false desires and needs.

Thus the humanistic revolution seeks to rescue the positive qualities of life experience; it seeks to rediscover joy and love, creativity and growth, shared experiences and fraternity, uniqueness and diversity, achievement and excellence. These are human goods that must be cultivated anew if we are to overcome the blind forces that threaten the quality of life. A significant life, which fuses pleasure and creative self-realization, *is* possible, says the Humanist, and men can again discover ways of enriching experience, actualizing potentialities and achieving happiness. But if human experience is to flower it is essential that normative principles prevail in our social life.

Thus the new morality believes in moral liberation and freedom. This demand for moral freedom is part and parcel of the libertarian ethic; it has roots deep within the liberal tradition of Locke, Paine, Jefferson and Mill. Classical liberalism tended to focus primarily on political and civil liberty. It defended the rights of individuals to express their beliefs, choose their representatives in government and influence public policy.

Implicit in a system of values that prizes freedom high on the scale of human values, however, should be an equal concern for moral freedom. A just society is one that ought to allow individuals to satisfy their tastes, follow their careers, fulfil their moral and aesthetic visions and guide their own destinies as they see fit, without undue social pressure or governmental restriction.

Moral libertarianism expresses itself in many ways. There is today a more tolerant attitude toward sexual freedom and a demand that laws against abortion, birth control and voluntary sterilization be repealed. There is a change in public attitudes towards pornography and obscenity, in increased acceptance of nudity on stage and in the cinema—especially where artistic values are involved—and in a conviction that society should not impose narrow standards of censorship. There is also a more liberal attitude

51

towards the vagaries of sexuality. Sexual relations between consenting adults should be beyond the range of the law. Although drug use worries many people, libertarianism has also had some effect in modifying attitudes in this area. Many hold the view, for example, that marijuana should be legalized, or at least that severe penalties against possession and use be reduced.

Moral libertarianism can be positive in impact, for it suggests that a mature society should be tolerant of the wide diversity in human values and that it should avoid the uniform imposition of narrow puritanical restrictions upon all humans. It is interesting to note that both conservatives and radicals have found a common meeting ground in espousing the ideal of libertarianism.

The libertarian demand may assume ridiculous form. If pushed to extremes, it may lead to a flaunting of all standards of decency and propriety; freedom may degenerate into irresponsible and uncivilized behaviour. But moral libertarianism need not so degenerate. The principle can play a vital rôle in emancipating individuals from group oppression and in helping to create a humane society. If used with moderation and balance, the principle allows for the development of a reasonable and responsible approach toward life. A mature person recognizes that he can tolerate divergent life styles without necessarily approving of them. In so doing, the horizons of his own personality may be broadened and enriched.

Another principle that is pivotal in the present-day moral revolution is the demand for equal rights, the search for community. It is clear that an individual's freedom can be seriously impaired if he is denied equal treatment by society. Many minority groups have been oppressed. Blacks, Chicanos, and Indians have been submerged and discriminated against, are unable to share in the goods of the affluent society and have had their freedom of choice and fulfilment impaired. Thus the principle of equality is appealed to in order to help the poor achieve some measure of happiness. It has also been invoked to gain equal treatment for women, students, prisoners, homosexuals and other groups in society who have been denied their equal rights.

The principle of equality is a basic principle of the democratic ethic. Those who appeal to it in a society that professes to be democratic, yet often is not, indict the disparity between democratic ideals and actual deeds. No individual can be free if he is denied certain elementary human rights. An unjust society is one in which there are obstacles placed in the path of human realization. When this condition exists, the only recourse may be social reform.

A paradox of the moral life is that the equality principle, like the libertarian principle, can be misused. There is often great confusion as to what the principle implies and how it should be interpreted. If it is abused, individual liberty may be destroyed. The principle of equality should not be equated with egalitarianism. It does not maintain that all men are born equal in talent and capacity. Rather it recognizes the existence of biological and cultural inequalities and it admits differences in individual ability. The principle is not descriptive of what men are, but prescriptive and normative of how they should be treated in the future.

The principle of equality involves at least three ancillary principles: first, that we should grant all human beings, who are equal in dignity and value, equality of consideration and equality of treatment; second, that we grant equality of opportunity by removing all false barriers impeding individual and group advancement; and third, wherever possible, that we satisfy the minimum basic economic and cultural needs of all human beings.

The principle of equality should not necessarily imply a levelling down. It should be sensitive to the plurality of human needs and to the diverse means that may be required for their satisfaction. Nor should the principle mean the destruction of standards of excellence. Thus, for example, while all men should have equal opportunity to apply for admittance to a university or college (and, in my judgment, receive free scholarship tuition if they so qualify), this does not guarantee their admission if they lack talent, nor does it insure everyone the 'right' to graduate—unless, that is, they demonstrate their competence in performance. The danger of the equalitarian principle is that it will be indiscriminately misapplied by well-meaning moralists, and in the process destroy other meaningful moral principles and values. If properly understood and used, however, the principle can contribute immeasurably to the humanization of life and the development of a genuine community based on trust and co-operation.

Another important principle that has a powerful appeal today is participatory democracy. According to this principle, individuals ought to have some decision over their lives, that is, power ought to be extended to those who are affected by it. 'Power to the people'

53

is a slogan that has usually been applied to political democracy: it has meant that governments ought not to govern without the consent of the governed. The moral revolution has now extended the democratic ethic and the ideal of participation to other institutions in society: to the school, church, economy, voluntary associations and organizations of all kinds. It claims that we need to democratize our institutions, to make them amenable and responsive to the views of those within them. Participatory democracy has thus become a new frontier for social reform.

The principle of participatory democracy was perhaps the most significant contribution to come out of the early Port Huron Statement (1962) of the SDS—which at its inception was full of humanistic idealism. Unfortunately, moral ideals often degenerate into mere rhetorical slogans; and participatory democracy has suffered this fate. The demand for participation needs to be balanced against the need to maintain standards of excellence. Democracy should not be construed as preventing those who have talent and competence from exercising leadership. To say this does not commit one to an anti-democratic 'elitist' position. How participation works out—in the university, the hospital, the corporation—must be determined in each separate institution, in its own way, so as not to destroy the ability of the institution to function.

Participatory democracy, like liberty and equality, is a vital moral principle. It recognizes that the more human beings can take part in their own institutions, the better their quality of life experience, and the less their chance of alienation.

A word of caution: moral principles when first enunciated may give way to uncritical fervour and passion. There is a tendency for men to be misled or trapped by their moral commitments, to be overwhelmed by fashionable sloganeering. There is always the danger of a new religious romanticism being proclaimed indiscriminately, without reference to the complexities, subtleties and nuances involved in moral choice. There are many moral principles other than the above that have claims upon our conscience: peace, co-operation, excellence, achievement, reason, courage and tolerance are some of them. Any one set of principles must be evaluated and balanced in relationship to other principles and values that we cherish. Principles must be judged by how well they work out in practice, how they function in the concrete situations of life

54

experience. In the last analysis, rhetoric must not become a substitute for clarity, nor passion for thought.

Surely we need to reconstruct the moral conceptions we have inherited from a previous age. This reconstruction should be humanistic, that is, it should be predicated upon a concern for individual human beings and their needs. But we must guard our new moral principles to prevent their degeneration into forms of moral mysticism or absolutism.

Compassionate feeling is an essential human good that has a rightful place in human affairs. But it should not be in opposition to reason, rather in unity and harmony with it. A critical morality is one that questions basic assumptions, yet is committed to the use of critical intelligence. Accordingly, moral principles should be treated as hypotheses, tested by how they work out in practice and judged by their actual consequences. They need to be hammered out on the anvil of reason, not fed by the fires of neoprimitive passion. If so approached, the moral revolution can truly help to create a better life for all men.

9
Ethical Humanism
EDWARD L. ERICSON

E THICAL HUMANISM is a philosophy and moral faith founded upon the twin principles of human responsibility and personal worth. While uniformity of belief is not characteristic of ethical Humanists, most affirm moral responsibility (based upon the assumption of freedom of choice) as a genuine human capacity that education, religion and the social order must seek to maximize.

Authentic moral freedom derives from the nature and creative activity of man himself, from the interplay of his social feeling and rationality (the ability to foresee consequences and consider conflicting ends) combined with the drive to achieve meaning and wholeness in personal and social life. Thus, man is a goal-seeking organism whose values can never be treated as purely arbitrary or accidental, however conflicted or distorted they may be, since they arise from needs and relationships grounded in the realities of human life and history.

Moral problems are therefore *real* problems; man's dignity, as William James saw, consists in his fighting what he rightly experiences as a real battle over genuine moral stakes. The substantial and rational character of our deepest and most enduring values enables the ethical Humanist to live in the rational belief that he is dealing with goods that are objective without the further claim of their being absolute, and that are relative (relational) without the false inference of their being merely subjective. The ethical Humanist finds his 'golden mean' in an earth-born, life-centred and realistic ethic—open, empathic, pragmatic and nonexclusive—enabling us to avoid the extremes of absolutism and nihilism, which are alike corrosive of meaningful freedom and responsibility.

Ethical Humanist views are held widely among educators, religious liberals, secularists and theorists of democratic life. Especially the philosophical heirs and successors of William James,

F. C. S. Schiller, John Dewey, Morris R. Cohen and related thinkers subscribe to variations of the same outlook.

As social thinkers and activists, ethical Humanists stress an ethic that emphasizes the interdependence of cultural and social systems, the equality of races and the values of open political and spiritual interchange. All subscribe to the use of democratic methods and the avoidance of authoritarian and terrorist means, whether exploited by left or right, which break down the relationships and trust upon which mutual help and civilized standards rest.

As the ideological battleline has shifted from the now largely moribund claims of fundamentalist and authoritarian religion to the sanguinary assaults of political totalitarianism upon liberal values and standards, ethical Humanists have become increasingly able to work with democratic and progressive churchmen, as with secular educators and reformers, to effect social change within the orderly processes of constitutional democracy. The future of this irenic and mediatory ethic, like so much else of humanistic value in civilization, hinges upon the efficacy of orderly and democratic procedures as instruments of social reconstruction.

10

What is the
Temper of Humanism?

JOHN HERMAN RANDALL JR.

HUMANISM IS A CERTAIN RELIGIOUS TEMPER, a certain set of values. It involves an attitude toward, and an appraisal of, the nature and possibilities of man and his essential needs. The Humanist temper is difficult to define satisfactorily. Those sharing the Humanist temper would view religion as primarily devotion to the ideals discoverable in human experience and would rely on man's efforts, in co-operation with the natural resources he finds in his world, to bring these ideals measurably into existence. The Humanist temper holds that men should place their faith in man himself—in man's infinite possibilities. This faith should, of course, be coupled with a realistic recognition of man's infinite limitations—of man's capacities for 'sin', for falling short of the highest he has seen. In a word, the faith in intelligence and in man is Humanism.

Let us try again on a deeper and more universal level. Let us consider a thoughtful and reflective statement made recently. This runs: 'The Humanist temper is man's awareness of a sense of human dignity and power, and of a sense of responsibility for cultivating and maintaining it, and for achieving an integrity and wholeness of human life.' (Definition given by Horace L. Friess.)

I will comment on certain aspects of this statement, to bring out the major factors in the Humanist temper, the chief values involved and the conception of the nature of man it implies. There is, in the first place, an emphasis on the power and dignity of man, on the worth of human personality. There is, secondly, an emphasis on the obligation to respect and cultivate that dignity and worth in oneself and in others. And there is, thirdly, an emphasis on responsibility, on self-control, on self-direction towards integrity and wholeness as the foundation on which the others rest.

Of these three factors, the underlying one, responsibility, implies that in some meaningful human sense man is free. The Humanist temper has always protested against any subservience to an external law, whether religious or mechanical, imposed upon man from without. But at the same time, 'obligation' means that insofar as man recognizes that obligation, he is not wholly free. The very essence of the moral life is bondage. Obligation is a curtailment of the freedom to do wrong. Both freedom and obligation are united in the notion of self-control.

The reconciliation of freedom and obligation, both intellectual and practical, is a complex, ever-shifting, never 'solved' problem, for it involves all that men have experienced and all that they have come to know about their life in the world. Man is free only insofar as what used to be called reason and has now been reconstructed into intelligence is free to discover truth—especially truth about what is good. In the measure that intelligence is free—and how small that measure is, historically, socially and institutionally, is notorious—man can hope to determine his will by knowledge rather than by ignorance. The practical human problem is to increase this freedom of reason or of intelligence—the determination of intelligence by truth and good—and, by so increasing it, to minimize freedom of the will, the freedom to choose the wrong and the bad.

The second factor in the Humanist temper is the obligation to respect and cultivate the dignity and worth of human personality, in oneself and in others. Men have always asked why we should hold that human personality is inviolable. We Westerners have come to share that moral commitment to the worth of human personality, whatever the reasons we may assign for it, and whatever our actual practice may have been, or may continue to be. Every great moral and social movement in the West has been inspired by some form of that conviction. Such a basic moral commitment seems to be rooted in man's long ethical experience. That experience is very complex. Ethical experience includes the way in which the long embodiment of men's past encounters with life comes home to us—in that profound revulsion that occurs when we confront what comes to us as an instance of injustice and violation, when we cry out in vivid realization, 'But that is wrong!'. The Humanist temper tends to take such moral experience as primary and basic. The Humanist temper would insist on the autonomy of the moral life.

There remains the factor in the Humanist temper we listed first,

59

'a sense of human dignity and power'. Of the many powers of man exercised in co-operation with those of the world in which he finds himself, I should like to make central here the power of self-criticism —a power equally exercised in co-operation with the powers of man's world, that is, of a world that displays to man an ethical dimension. Thinking of the patron saint of reason and philosophy, we might call this human power of self-criticism the Socratic power. It is man's power to examine his life in the light of those ideals that, as Socrates put it, are 'deathless and divine'. It is the power of using what the Greeks called *nous*, and what we today should call a combination of imagination, vision and intelligence, to increase man's moral wisdom to deal with the facts of wrong, injustice and evil in his life. It is man's power to use the vision of Good to achieve a moral perspective that will enable him to deal with and rise above the facts of evil and sin. It is clear that there will always be some limits to what human nature can become. At the same time, it is likewise clear that no specific limit can be found in human nature that is immutable and cannot be pushed back. The prospect seems to be for bigger and better sins; or rather, if we are very optimistic, for more refined, and perhaps for that very reason, more corrosive sins. For the increasing complexity of our social organization involves multiplying opportunities for twisted and tangled relations between men.

Man's power of self-criticism, his power of seeing himself in a broader perspective, enables him to go beyond the Stoic attitude of sheer endurance in meeting and dealing with inevitable evil. It makes it possible for him to take that evil as a challenge to reveal his nature as a man, as a moral personality capable of using evil as an instrument to further growth of character and insight and vision.

Men need a vision of a moral ideal that will transcend their finite ends. They need an end for living that can stand against outward frustration and failure and serve as an incentive toward striving for victory against insuperable odds—a victory that will not, like merely finite and temporal goods, turn to dust and ashes in the grasp. With such a vision men can wrest victory out of the very jaws of defeat. For in disaster, finite ends are revealed as finite and man sees himself in his true stature as what we call a 'spiritual' being. Living as he must within the narrow limits of time and space, he can yet behold a vision that raises him above those limits, and above the petty conditions of existence, and reveals at once his weakness and his greatness. That revelation is the very essence of tragedy. Tragedy has always appeared as the supreme creative achievement of the human spirit, the supreme illustration of the human power of self-criticism.

I have been discussing the nature and destiny of man, human freedom and human obligation and self-control, ethical experience and spiritual vision. They are the main strands, I submit, of the temper of Humanism.

IV RELIGION AND HUMANISM

11
Religious Humanism
HERBERT W. SCHNEIDER

THE TERM RELIGIOUS HUMANISM covers and confuses two quite different matters: Humanism as a religion and religion interpreted as a form of human expression and art.

Humanist religion is primarily an effort to free religious faith and devotion from the dogmas of theistic theologies and supernaturalist psychologies. Because Humanists assume (or conclude from bitter experience) that contemporary religious institutions are committed to these theologies and psychologies, they regard themselves as necessarily anti-clerical, laic or secular. As a result of their alienation from religious institutions, their conceptions of religious experience are usually individualistic and they hesitate to establish a sect or a religious organization. They may make their Humanist faith articulate by formulating a creed, but they avoid religious rites. Nevertheless, being usually on the defensive, they insist stoutly that their faith is religious and their devotion authentic even though they do not use rituals or conventional forms of worship and devoutness. They also cultivate an informal fellowship and co-operate in defence and in anti-clerical preaching. They are a militant minority whose righteous indignation and confessed reasonableness prompt them to confront organized religious bodies that cherish theistic beliefs and supernatural devotions.

Humanist interpretations of religion have a longer history and usually have operated as reform movements within particular religions, but they have become increasingly radical with the relatively recent growth of a genuine science of religion, on which Humanists depend. Humanism attempts to rid religious institutions, myths, creeds, prayers and sacraments of superstitious beliefs, while enhancing their significance as expressions of human needs, hopes and values. This goal has led Humanists into elaborate, critical analyses of religious experience, ecclesiastical forms and mythical

c

expression. Assuming that a religion is neither true nor false as a whole, Humanists attempt to make a critical evaluation of religions and to determine when and how religions are good or evil. It becomes necessary to explore the imaginative arts and metaphorical languages of myths, creeds, rites and prophesies. Such exploration involves a study of the relation between sacred and secular arts, languages and devotions; it becomes critical of a devoutness that is pernicious, parasitical or childish. It is an inevitable extension of the arts of criticism and has an important function in promoting civilized behaviour and intelligent thought. Like other arts and philosophies, it runs the danger of becoming narrow, dogmatic or fashionable; and therefore religious Humanists should be religiously alert to criticise each other as well as religion.

12
Humanistic Theism
GARDNER WILLIAMS

M ANY HUMANISTS reject God's existence and all theories of world purpose. Many Humanists think that religion ought to be abolished because it is fraudulent. But other Humanists think that they need a rationally trustworthy religious-inspirational element to replace the old myths. I believe that we should retain our scientific standards and sound critical scholarship in dealing with ancient documents, including the Bible; by now we should all be able to recognize primitive supernaturalistic mythology when we see it. We should also cultivate a passionate devotion to the great ideal of man's highest good. Moreover, we should communicate all this not only to disoriented youth, but also to as many of their spiritually-troubled elders as care to listen.

But, various people will ask, can we cultivate such devotion when we truthfully deny the existence of God? Is spiritual inspiration possible without falsehood? Recently the Fellowship of Religious Humanists in Yellow Springs, Ohio, has been attempting to demonstrate that it is; the American Ethical Union has also tried, with some success, ever since its inception in 1876.

Humanists seldom proclaim publicly the nonexistence of God or openly endorse atheism. These expressions are emotionally charged. Asserting them may lead to one's complete social rejection and consequent defeat in every creative effort. They are commonly taken to be an endorsement of utter moral depravity.

David Hume, T. H. Huxley and Robert Ingersoll all knew that God does not exist, but they never said so. They said they were sceptics or agnostics. They said they did not know whether He existed or not. One should try to survive, prosper and contribute creatively even in a society that makes perverse and imperious demands.

I would like to propose some ideas and a terminology that,

hopefully, will allow for both honesty and social acceptance. They are suggested in George Santayana's *Reason in Religion*.[1] Here two traditional meanings of the word 'God' are indicated. One is the basic physical cosmic *substance* and unintentional creative force. The other is the *ideal* of the highest good, the *summum bonum*, the goal of man's ultimate rational devotion, aspiration, striving and commitment. In Christian theology, says Santayana, 'the grand contradiction is the idea that the same God who is the ideal of human aspiration is also the creator of the universe and its only primary substance.'[2]

In order to avoid this muddled ideology, I suggest that we call the basic physical substance of the cosmos the *supreme being*, and save the word God for the ideal of man's highest good. The supreme being is omnipotent. It has, or is, all power and all force. It participates in and produces all actual events. It does everything that is done, both good and evil. We should be piously grateful to it for all our blessings. It has, creatively and mostly unintentionally caused life, consciousness, purpose, reason and all the grandeur and the glory that man has ever experienced. But it has also caused frustration, despair, anguish, suffering and death. Whatever causes evil is instrumentally evil. And the worship of evil is idolatrous.

God is something else again. As to His cosmic status, Santayana has some enlightening suggestions. God, he says, is a potential, not an actual or substantial being. He, She or It never exists. Nevertheless He is a real fact, since He is something about which one can tell the truth. The truth is that God, the highest good, ought to exist because people would be so much happier if He were actualized in their lives. *Truth* should be defined as a statement about some fact when the fact is exactly as stated. This truth that I have stated about God can be a truth only if God is a fact that is exactly as here stated. So God must be a real, factual nonexistent potential. Santayana[3] uses the word 'subsist', in contrast with 'exist', for Its mode of being. Real things, beings, facts or entities which subsist only as mere potentials, he calls 'essences'. God is a real essence, not an actual substance or the actual attribute of any substance.

The brain is an actually existing and highly evolved substance. The idea or thought of God is occasionally an actual attribute of it.

[1] Santayana, George (1905), *Reason in Religion*, New York: Charles Scribner's Sons, chapters 6, 9, 10, 11.

[2] *op. cit.*, p. 159.

[3] Santayana, George (1923), *Scepticism and Animal Faith*, New York: Charles Scribner's Sons.

God is an essence that ought to be actualized but never is in this vale of tears, this world of sin and sorrow. Lesser goods, of course, are constantly being actualized in us and all about us. They and we ought to be as God-like as possible. This is the practical application of our Humanistic Theism, which we should try to embody in the tradition of the liberal Churches.

God and the supreme being are, in principle, a whole universe apart. There is nothing lower than the supreme being and nothing higher than God. The supreme being is the substance that underlies all actual occurrences and God is an ideal above all human achievement. The whole duty of man is to make the actual conform as nearly as possible to the ideal.

Consider another important potential essence. In every society there is a vast criminal potential that ought not to be actualized. Usually the actual penal systems of police, courts, jails, poison gas chambers etc., keep most of it out of existence. But in great disasters like floods, earthquakes, city-wide conflagrations and aerial bombings, this potential essence has been in large measure actualized. Amid all the noise and confusion in the saturation bombing of Dresden, Saxony, in February 1945, when few residents could be arrested or punished for any crime, widespread looting and occasional murder by unidentified persons were reported as actually occurring.

The basic reason why so many people regard atheism as moral depravity is their subconscious assumption of the officially and rather widely-expressed view that, properly speaking, God is the principle or essence of the highest good. Man's first duty is to God. This, I say, is Humanistic Theism. To repudiate it in practice is moral depravity. To deny it is atheism. But it is neither.

13
Our Quest for Faith:
Is Humanism Enough?
ALGERNON D. BLACK

THE TRADITIONAL FAITHS are relatively recent in human history. The earth may be two billion years old. Man may have lived on this earth over a million years. In the long history of man, the polytheistic religious systems of the ancient Egyptians, Babylonians and Assyrians, of the Greeks and the Romans, go back not more than five to ten thousand years at the outside. Similarly, Hinduism, Buddhism, Shintoism and the faith of Islam, the choices of those in the Middle East and Asia, may seem ancient and venerable, but they, too, are relatively modern. In the West, the religion of Judaism is about 3,000 years old and Christianity only about 2,000 years old. In our world of emphasis on modernism and recent discovery and rapid change, these seem ancient; but the fact is that they are comparatively young in time.

Even so, many of their concepts are no longer relevant. Science and technology have changed our lives and our relationships to nature and to each other. Whereas many human communities once lived in relative isolation, now we are all close and interdependent neighbours. Whereas human beings once lived on a narrow margin, with a scarcity of the necessities of life, now we live with a productivity of abundant surplus. Whereas change in knowledge and power, in ideas and institutions was relatively slow, now we see change, rapid change, on every hand.

In the midst of the confusion and conflict of the modern world, men have lost their identity, have suffered alienation from their own feelings and from personal relationships and small communities. In many ways the individual feels alone and lonely, lost and helpless. Many have failed to find spiritual security and purpose and faith through traditional religious beliefs and affiliations. Many despair at ever finding any answers to their need for faith.

70

In the past, men inherited their faith and were indoctrinated with the faith of a particular community and time and place. A number of human needs led men to imagine and create the beliefs, doctrines and myths of the religions of primitive peoples and of the more developed civilizations. The need for some explanation of Creation, of the origin and purpose of life; the need for believing that they could tap some source of power for survival and reproduction and fertility; and the need for some belief about death—these evoked the religious life of every community.

How should we seek and find a faith to live by today? Shall we look to the faith of our fathers? Shall we be bound by what they believed? Shall we accept the idea that religious freedom means the right to believe only the way our ancestors believed? Is any departure from their faith to be taken as a lack of loyalty or lack of respect of one's elders? If we accept this, then the concept of religious freedom is severely limited.

Recently I met a group of children of junior high school age. They were from homes in the Humanist tradition. I asked the children how many believed in God. There was an almost unanimous silence. 'Is there no one here who believes in God?' I asked. Finally, a child put up his hand. Then another raised her hand cautiously, saying, 'I'm only a visitor. I am a Catholic.'

'What do you mean by God?' I asked. 'I know it's a personal question and most people don't ask it. But do you know the meaning or do you have any idea about what you mean by the God you *believe* in? And for those who don't believe, do you have any idea of what you mean by the God you *don't believe* in?'

The first child who put up his hand said, 'Well, there must have been somebody who made the world.' He was saying the same thing as those who through the thousands of years have asked and made answers. So the priest had said many times: 'Do you see this watch? Where there is a watch there must be a watchmaker.' Yes, something in the human brain responds to the idea of cause and effect. There must be a cause—and a cause *of* the cause—and a cause *of all* the causes, a first cause. So also the priest or the rationalist may argue, 'Here is a watch. The watch is more than mere metal and glass, a face and hands. The watch was made for a purpose. And there is a purpose to the purpose, an end beyond the end.'

But beyond this dry logic and thin rational approach are other, deeper factors. These include the psychological needs for security,

71

for protection—for a father, law-giver, judge, protector, for one who will be punishing and forgiving.

More and more human beings throughout the world have been moving away from fixed and final definitions concerning an ultimate reality or the absolute dogma of a God who created and rules the universe. More and more people are sceptical of an all-powerful, all-knowing, all-merciful, all-just and all-loving God. Many would say, 'If there were such a power, such a God, how could He permit the cruelty, waste and suffering of the world?' And many are no longer satisfied with 'You must take it on faith. There are things beyond human understanding. Trust! Believe! God and His ways are infinite. Man is limited and finite. You cannot grasp the larger truth. Have faith!'

Now if there is one thing that human beings want to believe, if there is one idea that most men have of God—no matter how they differ in language and theology and culture—it is this: that God is a power which will make everything come out all right in the end. He is a power that makes for righteousness. He guarantees that good will win over evil, peace over war, justice over injustice, love over hate. Most people would like to believe that the universe is weighted at least 51 per cent in favour of goodness. Most people want to believe that no matter what happens to them or their loved ones and no matter what happens to their dreams, aspirations and values, somehow there is a guarantee of victory. They want to believe that there is a built-in guarantee that no matter what mistakes or evils men may do, there is a power at the heart of things which will assure that life is sustained both in life and in death. And the hunger and the longing for such assurance evokes the belief, makes it easy for man to affirm and teach and build institutions which structure and reinforce a faith.

Now we would all like to have evidence that there is such a tendency and support for what human beings value as moral and ethical. But there is no evidence. When the lightning strikes; when the earthquake swallows men, women and children; when the flood or famine or plague takes its toll, there is no evidence that nature discriminates and favours goodness. The universe appears untouched, impervious to human aspiration, dreams, values, visions.

Do the people who believe that evil will be defeated and the evildoers punished, question why there is so much crime, so much inhumanity among men—the killing, robbing, betrayal, violation of human beings? There is no evidence that those who believe in the traditional God concepts are more law-abiding or respecting of their fellows or considerate of society than those who have turned from theism. Obviously, more and more human beings all over the world have lost their faith—if they ever really had it beyond lip-service or rather thin and vague concepts.

Thus the quest for faith must go beyond the God belief. Man has to face the fact that he does not know the beginning of the beginnings and that he does not know the purpose, and the purpose beyond all purposes, of the universe. We are all a part of some larger reality or cosmos, some process beyond our grasp. And we live in a natural world in a condition of limited knowledge and power. We sense that there are still vast areas for man's investigation. We will certainly increase our knowledge of the reality of the universe in the time before the human organism made its appearance in the evolutionary process. We may reach out into space in our solar system and even beyond it. We may penetrate further the nature of the atom and the living cell. Most important of all is the exploration of our own psychological and spiritual natures and the inter-relationships of life with life. But we must not permit ourselves to stop growing or to accept the dogmas and horizons of the past as the limits of our thought. And whether we seek new symbols beyond a God or Saviour, beyond a Revelation or Salvation, or whether we remain with the old, we cannot expect to fulfil the human distinctiveness of our species unless we recognize the need for growth and development, the possibilities and potentialities of growth in the individual and in the quality of human relations and in the nature of human society.

Thus, instead of feeling confused and lost and bereft, deprived of faith, we can find that the quest for faith means a new challenge, a new sense of possibilities beyond any of the visions of the past. The Humanist does not fall into the trap of believing that man is the superpower, the highest form of life in existence. Man may be the highest form we know. But the universe does not revolve around man, nor does it necessarily exist for man. All man can do in seeking a faith is to be honest in examining his world of natural environment and his human environment and, above all, in examining himself. Out of human experience man gains a sense of life's possibilities and the choices before him in his personal life, his patterns of relationships and the kinds of community he may strive for. And with the

73

awareness of man's potentialities and the choices before him, man faces challenge, opportunity and responsibility.

And it is at this point that we have to face up to the intelligence potentials, the aesthetic aspects and ethical elements in the human being. As far as we can see a vital drive is built into the lower forms of insect and animal life; it is part of the will to survive. Admittedly, an animal, bird or fish, may reach a point at which it can no longer fight or fend for itself or perform its natural physical functions. It is finished. Maybe there is some beyond-physical sense of impending death. But we do not know this as surely as we know the phenomenon in humans. We doubt that lower forms of life have a problem of faith.

For humans, uncertainty about whether or not to believe in particular doctrines is a part of the problem. But whether to believe in life, whether life is worth living and whether there is any meaning in some larger reality beyond the life of the individual and beyond the entire human enterprise—these are the real dilemmas for human beings. True, many men may never become aware of these problems. They live their lives on certain levels and die when the time comes with seeming comfort from inherited beliefs which they have never questioned or dared to question. But more and more human beings, sensitive to suffering and waste of human potential, more and more human beings sensitive to the intellectual or aesthetic or ethical possibilities are doubting, asking, seeking.

We all feel futility and despair at certain times. 'Is life worth living?' asked William James. He answered, 'It depends on the liver.' And so it does. But it also depends on us living together and how we live together. It depends on how we help each other feel about life. For in and through our relationships we can hurt or help. We can rob a person of the taste for life and the will to live. We can permit or create conditions in which human beings are doomed to death from illness, doomed to distrust and bitterness toward each other, doomed to self-rejection and self-destruction. And on the other hand, we can create relations and conditions which foster the taste for life, the will to live and the hunger for creativeness and love.

Humanism calls men to shed the dogmas and divisions of traditional religion. Humanism calls man to face the fact that we must live without an absolute guarantee of victory for our values. Humanism calls men to awareness of human possibilities and the choices and the responsibilities before the human individual and the human community.

Nature, with all its wonder and beauty and miraculous creative powers, is also cruel. The meadow, so beautiful with grass and flowers, with busy birds and insects, may inspire the artist and the poet with romance and dreams. But when we look more carefully, we see life feeding on life. Among the rocks and behind the flowers and under the earth, life forms are killing other life forms. What may be 'natural' in the behaviour of some of the forms of insect and bird life, among the organisms in the sea and jungle, is found also among humans. But in the evolution of human life, there is a consciousness and emerging conscience. The key question is whether human beings can rise to a level of awareness of the values and the choices which are within human control.

The forces of nature which are beyond man's control, the earthquakes and floods and tidal waves can be studied and offset within limits by human ingenuity. What we cannot control or do anything about should not be a source of worry or anxiety. But what is within human control, human beings had better face and deal with. Earthquakes triggered by extreme explosive forces due to nuclear explosions set off by man cannot be blamed on nature. The same applies to human carelessness in causing pollution of the earth, air or water by chemicals and radiation. Humanism does not mean that man is omnipotent. But it does mean that man must be responsible for his uses of the knowledge and the power he has won through thousands of years of intelligent study of his environment.

The important question is: 'What does man make of himself?' With the resources of earth and the knowledge and power human beings now have it is not enough to survive, to exist, to be a vegetable or an animal with the capacity to breathe, eat, defecate and reproduce its kind. There is a new level of responsibility for achieving a quality of life, a quality of being and a level of consciousness and creativeness beyond anything man has thus far achieved in intellectual and aesthetic and ethical potentialities.

Many men will say they cannot live without a guarantee of victory for the best in human values, that they cannot live without a faith in another life, that they cannot live without the perfectability of man in society—that Humanism is not enough. So, too, they will say they cannot live without fixed and final doctrines. We deny this. The central problem is an ethical problem. Humanism may include the intellectual, rational, logical and scientific dimensions of man; it may include the aesthetic, sensitivity to beauty, nature and civilization; but it must also include the deep and rich emotional and spiritual elements which are part of man's relationships—the affection, compassion, the identification and the love which is a potential in human beings in all the relations of life. This is a many-dimensional Humanism. It is with this perspective that we call human beings to seek out and fulfil their highest potentialities.

Men cannot live without hope. Men cannot live without faith. Hope has to do with a sense that something better is possible. Hope may include a desire and a wish in the midst of uncertainty. But faith has more strength than hope. It is a call to commitment, a readiness to strive, sacrifice, stake a life on an outcome and a fulfilment. To have faith is to have a sense of values worth living for; to try to be faithful to an ideal or a vision of possibilities.

And the quest for faith depends on the attitude that men do not give up, do not yield to the darkness, do not yield to the seemingly overwhelming tough realities. It requires that men assume that they may have the capacity to think through their difficulties and overcome their obstacles. It is a quest for clarification of purpose and meaning which will give focus to life. It is a process by which men grow through seeking and striving.

Humanism has hope and faith for man. But it makes no false promises. No one can live a perfect life. No one can fulfil his powers and gifts completely. There is not a single individual who will grow to the full use of all his intelligence. And every day millions die who have not learned to fulfil all their powers to appreciate and enjoy or create beauty. And many will never have had the experience of being loved or loving. We use only a fraction of our potentials. This is the human tragedy. And it is revealed most in our failure to achieve greater fulfilment in and through our relationships. None of us is good enough. We all fall short at some point in friendship, in understanding and loving and in being just to others.

Humanism does not hold that man is perfect or perfectable. No one who has ever lived has lived a perfect life nor will it occur in the future. All our fulfilments are partial—greater in some and less in others.

And no society is perfect or perfectable either. Will man ever achieve a truly free and just society? Will the dream of democracy ever be fulfilled perfectly? When we say to children that no man is perfectable and no society will ever be perfect, we may say, 'An individual may come near it. A society may come near it. There may be moments in the lives of individuals and periods in communities when they come very near fulfilment of their promise. But there are no saints and there are no Utopias.' And when we say this, the child asks, 'Then what's the use of trying to be a better person? What's the use of trying to work for a better world?'

How shall we answer? It may be that we have to say that the important thing is not the finished product, the perfect individual or the perfect society. The value lies in what we try to be and try to do and what happens to us in the striving. Perhaps it is in that process that we grow and mature. Perhaps it is man's fate to strive even though he knows that he will never fulfil his dream of self and his dream of society. We are not children asking for an easy and cheap gift. We are not content to live with illusions that fulfilment is guaranteed or that our effort will bring us some sweet reward from outside of man. No. Man stands on his own feet without fear of punishment or promise of reward. Man makes his own Hell and his own Heaven, and he makes it here and now.

Is the vision of partial fulfilment enough? Is it enough to say that the important result of striving for the fulfilment of man's many dimensions is the effect on himself, the by-product is greater inner security, greater self-esteem, greater dignity and freedom and the knowledge that man shapes his own destiny?

When we say this we are aware of our failures, our fears and hates, our wars and racism, and our unreadiness to share the gifts of nature and the human gifts, the riches of man's creative achievements. Some will say that Humanism is not enough, that it cannot satisfy, that it cannot generate in man the powers he needs to deal with and overcome the difficulties of his condition and his life. Others may say, 'Humanism is too much. It asks and demands too much from man.' But in our quest, let us say of ourselves and of others:

> Much in each of us is unexpected and mysterious
> Each of us is more than his thoughts
> In our love we seek our own perfection.
> So when you criticize the world of men
> Be gentle.
> Love, to abide, must not demand too much,
> We are trying to learn to live.

V ATHEISTIC HUMANISM

14
Heretical Humanism
MIRIAM ALLEN deFORD

IT IS PERHAPS unfortunate that the term Humanism was ever adopted for a humanity-centred philosophy; the word had already had a long and honourable career as denominating the renewed interest in the ancient classics and the humanities that came with the Renaissance. 'Rationalism' or 'secularism' would have been much more precise. Either of them, of course, would have barred out the religiously-oriented, but that, in my opinion, would have been desirable rather than disadvantageous.

However, as the American association took over that word in 1933 and as it has been more or less accepted also by our British colleagues, exact definitions have become necessary.

My own tentative general definition of Humanism as a whole would be that it is a philosophical system based on the concept that the universe, life and consequently mankind are the result of natural evolutionary processes alone, and hence that our view of them must be monistic. In other words, there is nothing in existence except random, fortuitous forces which eventually—in the manner of the famous example of the monkeys pounding typewriters who finally emerge with the works of Shakespeare—bring together consonant elements from which under favourable circumstances, galaxies, planetary systems, bacteria and human beings gradually issue and evolve.

Ethical Humanism can best be defined in the words of an anonymous pre-Confucian Chinese philosopher of the tenth century: 'Man must look in his own heart to know what he must do.' Or, to quote Robert G. Ingersoll, 'The accumulated experience of the world is a power and force that works for righteousness. This force is not conscious, not intelligent. It is a result.' It is the task of Humanism to show that ethics is a by-product of human experience, not of some supernatural mandate. Man must learn to exercise a high ethical

81

policy toward the earth on which he lives, toward the multitudinous plants and animals inhabiting it with him, toward his fellow humans—yes, and toward himself as well—or cease to survive.

Scientific Humanism in my thinking *is* Humanism; the general definition I have given above predicates a scientific approach to every philosophical, ethical and intellectual problem. This is not nineteenth century mechanistic materialism; there are many aspects of proved or provable reality (for example extrasensory perception) that we do not yet understand, but that are still phenomena susceptible to investigation and understanding.

Religious Humanism (*pace* the 'liberal religionists') is to me merely a contradiction in terms. Religion in its strict meaning implies belief in nonhumanistic systems, entities or explanations. A philosophy founded on the agreement that 'man is the measure of all things' can have no room for belief in the intervention of nonmaterial postulates. Conceivably, one might say that a person who believes that nothing exists but spirit is as much of a monist as a person who believes that nothing exists but natural, material phenomena. The one thing the adherent to either faith cannot be is a dualist, and religion by any definition is necessarily dependent on a dualistic order.

To put it bluntly and undiplomatically, Humanism, in my viewpoint, must be atheistic or it is not Humanism as I understand it. At the age of thirteen, I concluded that there is sufficient evidence that there are no gods, there is no soul, and there is no survival of personality after death. That was seventy-one years ago, and I have never heard any arguments since to cause me to negate that conclusion. I presume, in view of the wide orbit of belief among members of the American Humanist Association, that this makes me a heretical Humanist; nevertheless, as long as the orbit remains wide enough to include me, I shall still claim membership.

15

Aren't Humanists Really Atheists?

MARVIN ZIMMERMAN

Though the categories of Humanists and atheists do not coincide, their postures toward religion overlap significantly. Religious Humanists, like atheists, have usually given up on supernatural theology and morality. Nonetheless many Humanists disdain use of the term atheist, though their intellectual convictions about God are identical with, and constitute the very foundations of, the convictions of those who call themselves atheists. They have repudiated the belief in a perfect, omnipotent and benevolent creator who performs miracles, responds to prayer and proclaims a fundamental set of eternal moral principles. There is more than enough wretchedness in the world to justify overwhelmingly the tenet that if there were a deity, he would be either a devil or insane and this view is completely incompatible with any variety of theism that entails the existence of a benevolent and omnipotent God, however limited His characteristics.

Some Humanists disclaim atheism because they suppose it to be as dogmatic as theism. This is not even fair to theists, who, though mistaken, are not invariably dogmatic. There is no more reason to call oneself agnostic because one lacks absolute certainty in religious matters than there is to call oneself agnostic because one lacks absolute certainty in any other subject. The scientist does not allege to be agnostic toward the effectiveness of vaccines for smallpox and polio on the grounds that medical treatments merely possess high probability rather than absolute certainty. There is a fundamental difference between recognizing the possibility of error and being agnostic in believing that the available evidence is inconclusive.

Likewise, atheists do not necessarily consider themselves infallible or absolutely certain about their disbelief in God, any more than Humanists are about their support for Humanism and their rejection of supernatural values. In a scientific spirit characteristic of most Humanists, atheists can deny theism on the basis of high probability.

If Humanists are not convinced of the nonexistence of a traditional deity, why are they confident about the absence of absolute values, a major trait of Humanism? One can more rationally discredit theism than refute the presence of absolute or eternal values. Humanists who reject the reality of eternal or immutable values, acknowledge anti-absolutist attitudes. They have as much reason to accept anti-theist attitudes, that is, atheism. To be agnostic about the existence of a good and powerful creator, that is, to suggest that theism and atheism are equally plausible, given the adversities in this universe, makes less sense than to be agnostic about the reality of eternal or absolute moral principles. If a Humanist is positive (but not dogmatic) about the absence of the latter, then he has more reason to be positive about the absence of the former. It is far more unlikely that there is an all-powerful and all-good creator than that there are absolute moral values, which would perhaps be discovered if we only knew more about the nature of man, society and the universe.

Of course, atheism merely reflects a verdict about God, whereas the scope of Humanism extends to social, political and ethical values and scientific method. Thus, one would expect a greater percentage of Humanists to be atheists than *vice versa*. But even if all Humanists turned out to be atheists, unfortunately the converse is far from the truth. Some atheists reject the Humanistic values of democracy, freedom and scientific method which, to Humanists, are of immeasurably greater significance than disbelief in the existence of a Supreme Being.

Some Humanists decline the atheistic label in order to express their sense of priority over what is paramount. They deem theological questions inconsequential. But this is also true for many atheists who not only concede that ethical and political problems deserve prime attention, but that theological disputes may sidetrack more fundamental, mundane issues, such as war, freedom, poverty, racism and the like. In fairness to believers, some theists also acknowledge the secondary importance of theological differences. One must therefore distinguish between what one believes and what one believes is worthwhile, since the former contains many instances not falling within the latter.

A better life for humanity depends more on a human being's ethics than on his theology. This accounts for many believers and nonbelievers working together toward common goals, who are opposed by other devout and secular individuals likewise united in a common cause. Nevertheless, man's intelligence and critical faculties significantly effect his moral judgments. The Humanist who ignores the question of God's existence, or adopts an agnostic stance by refusing to accept the consequences of scientific evidence on theological issues, is likely to dilute the quality of his ethical conclusions.

Many Humanists admit they prefer not to suffer the pejorative use of the term atheist, though they agree intellectually with the atheist's position. Though perhaps not personally fearful, they think they can be more effective in winning support by not being identified as atheists. The pragmatic arguments for persuasive use of language do not change the fact that the Humanist who adopts this tactic is an atheist, though reluctant to designate himself one. At present, it is ironic that the Catholic Church is attempting to hold dialogue with atheists and that other religious groups do not hesitate to call themselves Christian or Jewish atheists, while some Humanists resist describing themselves as such. In the long run, it is doubtful that avoiding the atheist label outweighs being regarded as confused, ambiguous, evasive, hypocritical or dishonest.

VI PSYCHOLOGY,
SCIENCE AND HUMANISM

16
Reason with Compassion

H. J. EYSENCK

I T IS UNLIKELY THAT ALL HUMANISTS would agree on a definition of the term Humanism; what I shall do is simply to suggest what to me are the essentials of Humanism, without thereby trying to imply that others would necessarily agree. Indeed, I feel sure that old-fashioned Humanists, with the smell of bloody battles against religion still in their nostrils, will feel shocked at the cavalier disregard I may show for furthering such battles. I am strengthened, however, by my belief that at the bottom of Humanist attitudes lies belief in the power and importance of *reason*. Indeed, the REASON terms Humanist and rationalist used to be almost interchangeable. Opposition to religious beliefs was originally inspired by the fact that where Humanists put their faith in reason, religious people put their faith in faith. Thus, the first part of my definition of Humanism would involve a stress on the use of reason in dealing with inanimate nature and with other human beings. This inevitably involves the rejection of revealed religion and in that sense I am at one with old-fashioned Humanists.

I think that important differences arise when one attempts to extend the range of this definition beyond religion. All Humanists are agreed that religion is not based on reason, but not all Humanists would follow me in declaring that there are many other beliefs that are equally lacking in any rational basis. One such belief, for instance, is nationalism—that is, the belief that one's own nation is in some sense supremely endowed with all the good qualities of humankind, that one's nation has never waged an unjust war and that it must be supported through thick and thin. Political beliefs are also firmly held and may share with nationalism the doubtful honour of having replaced religion as the main stronghold of fervent but unreasoned support and faith. Socialism and capitalism both find their blind adherents even among people who ought to

89

know better; these kinds of people are incapable of subordinating the fervour of their political beliefs to the searching scrutiny of empirical research and factual investigation. Racism is another candidate for this modern rogues' gallery; many people hold very firm but inadequately based beliefs in the inferiority or superiority of one race with respect to other races. Finally, there are modern pseudo-religious belief systems (for example Communism, psychoanalysis) which are advertised as being scientific, but are no more so than the Church of Christ, Scientist. I believe that from the point of view of Humanism (or rationalism) these modern heresies are much more dangerous than religion. I believe that Humanists should be far more concerned with introducing the rule of reason into these fields than with fighting the old, long-won battles against religion all over again.

To young people nowadays, Humanism, like religion, wears a long Victorian beard and seems quite dated and irrelevant to modern problems. It seems to me that Humanism ought to update itself and turn to tasks more urgent than those which confronted it when religion was still strong and vicious. We might even find that modern religion is in many ways an ally rather than a foe. Ministers of many religions, for instance, have denounced South African doctrines of apartheid more strongly and loudly than Humanists have done, and the same is true of segregation in the southern states of the United States. Religion today in many respects is little but an ethical guide. Many officials of the various Churches would find difficulties in adhering to the thirty-nine Articles or in passing even minimum tests of religious orthodoxy. There are still relics of the Old Adam to be found, but on the whole it would seem to me that Humanists should look for worthier foes.

To me, the word reason in this respect implies science. Science is the embodiment of the rational attempt to solve problems posed by nature or by human beings in their variegated absurdity. Few people would deny that this is so with respect to physics, chemistry or astronomy; many would be surprised to hear it asserted with respect to psychology. Most of our problems nowadays, however, are psychological in origin—war, strikes and overpopulation are all caused by human beings, and failure to control the impulses that lead to these disastrous consequences is largely due to lack of scientific knowledge in the field of psychology. Yet we already possess a good deal of knowledge, laboriously acquired through laboratory investigations and the statistical analysis of empirically observed phenomena in everyday life. It should be the task of Humanists to make themselves familiar with such knowledge as exists already and to press for its use in the solution of human problems. Furthermore, Humanists should be in the forefront of those asking for the support of further research into these complex and difficult problems. It is not reasonable that we should waste a billion pounds on developing a plane that can transport an infinitesimally small number of people from London to New York in a slightly briefer period of time than has previously been required, but spend less than one quarter of 1 per cent of this sum annually on research in all the social sciences!

To my definition of Humanism I would add one further term: compassion. To me, Humanism is the use of reason in human affairs, applied in the service of compassion. Reason by itself does not set our aims, but provides merely the means through which our aims can be reached. It may be possible to develop a scientific ethic, that is, to prescribe our aims along purely rational lines. This has certainly been attempted by many wellknown persons. I am doubtful, however, whether such an attempt will succeed. Consequently I think that the addition of a qualifying clause, such as that suggested above, is needed. Reason can tell you that there is no scientific evidence to show that the Negroes transported as slaves to the United States were in any sense biologically inferior to their masters; reason by itself cannot tell you that whether these slaves were inferior, equal or superior to their captors, the very notion of slavery is obnoxious and must be eradicated. Any argument that purports to accomplish this conclusion along purely rational grounds will be found to be based on premises that themselves are taken as axiomatic and that prejudge the issue. I may be mistaken in this, but to me it seems that, at the present time at any rate, the addition of compassion to reason is needed if we want to make Humanism something other than a cold, selfish pursuit of a person's immediate self-interest through entirely rational means. A given slave-owner might argue—with reason!—that his own self-interest was best served by keeping his slaves working all day for him, by breeding genetically superior slaves from them through the application of genetic principles and by selling the resulting children at a good profit. Can reason disprove him? Reason, to me, marks out the method to be used on all occasions by Humanists; compassion marks out the ideal in the service of which reason is employed.

The revulsion many people nowadays feel against science illustrates well why, for me, reason alone cannot suffice as a definition of Humanism. Science, being the embodiment of reason, is equally capable of being employed in devising new medical methods of saving life and in devising new military methods of destroying life. Religion today is more clearly committed to compassion than are science and reason. Hence, I find it difficult to quarrel with religion (as an ethical rule) with the enthusiasm I would have felt 300 years ago when it arrogated to itself a position in which supernatural revelation was considered infinitely superior to reason. In rejecting religion altogether, Humanism may be throwing out the ethical baby with the supernatural bathwater. My definition of Humanism would try to reconcile these two fundamental contributions—reason and compassion—without both of which life on this planet is unlikely to continue and would be intolerable even if it did.

17
Toward
a New Humanism
FLOYD W. MATSON

THE QUESTION, 'What is Humanism?' is to all appearances the academic version of that overwhelming question which has taken two other traditional forms as well: a scientific version (What is man?) and an existential version (Who am I?). It was Max Scheler[1] who observed that in the twentieth century, for the first time, man became a problem to himself; it is a sobering thought, but Humanists know better. What is perceived as a problem in our technological society was recognized as a mystery by earlier cultures; in one vocabulary or another, the ontological question, the riddle of existence and the enigma of being, has risen to haunt us many times before. To be sure, it presents itself to consciousness as a burning issue only when, as today, there is a crisis of confidence in the prevailing theology and cosmology, which then becomes a crisis of identity. It is always a serious matter when the identity of man is called into question, a matter both ominous and hopeful: ominous because it betrays the presence of doubt and confusion, and hopeful because the very questioning may be again, as it has been once or twice before, a harbinger of renaissance and renewal.

To undertake a definition of Humanism is to attempt to make out the particular features of the human form and the human spirit which at a given moment appear most prominent and precious. NB The act of definition (or more exactly of self-definition) is therefore normative as well as descriptive; it not only points to something real, it points with pride and views with alarm. That which is thought to be most definitive of man—hence fundamental to Humanism—is that which is deemed most valuable and vulnerable

[1] Scheler, Max (1962), *Man's Place in Nature*, New York: Noonday, translated by Hans Meyerhoff.

as well as venerable. The question, What is Humanism?, is not, then, really academic at all; it is urgent, immediate, committed and (in the best sense of an abused term) relevant.

Surely it is all of that today. Not only Humanism and humaneness, but humanity itself, is in clear and present danger of extinction—on one side from the technology of violence, which has given us an irresistible armoury of doomsday machines and collective self-destructive devices; on the other side from the technology of industry, which has given us (as an accidental by-product of its enterprise) a chemical fallout which promises the slow death of the environment. Indeed, the physical threat to life and existence appears to many so compelling as to override all concerns and considerations other than that of survival itself. Ecologists, futurologists and behavioural strategists utter apocalyptic prophecies of the end of man qualified only by injunctions to embrace the faith and follow the mandates of the planned technetronic society—which proposes salvation by computer programming, systems analysis and biological engineering.

But the survival of humanity on such terms would not insure the survival of Humanism; quite the reverse. The values of the 'total society', whether cast in the abrasive mould of classic totalitarianism or in the crystal-palace form of the new industrial state, are antithetical to the values of Humanism by any reasonable or minimal definition of the term. Nor is it only the values of *1984*, of the putative future of our nightmares, which are in opposition to man; it is also the values of the 1970s, of the incorrigible present. The case against the present—that is, against the dominant imperatives of belief and value in our society—is familiar enough to those who read these pages to need no repetition.[2] The essence of the case is contained in Mumford's observation that, before the nineteenth century was over in America, 'the mechanical world picture took possession of the mind. It displaced both the natural world and cultural memory. It produced an environment in which

---

[2] For any who desire further instruction, the authoritative guidebooks are as follows: Mumford, Lewis (1970), *The Myth of the Machine: the Pentagon of Power*, New York: Harcourt, Brace and World; Muller, Herbert J. (1970), *The Children of Frankenstein: a Primer on Modern Technology and Human Values*, Bloomington, Indiana: Indiana University Press; Reich, Charles (1970), *The Greening of America*, New York: Random House; Fromm Erich (1968), *The Revolution of Hope: Toward a Humanized Technology*, New York: Bantam; Ellul, Jacques (1964), *The Technological Society*, New York: Knopf.

the technological complex—the Megamachine—became an end in itself, without regard for human needs and purposes.'[3]

If the Humanist case against the present on its overt technological side is generally well-known, the case against the present on its hidden subterranean side—its underlying image of man—is much less well-known. The tacit conception of human nature which supports the monolithic structures of the technological complex and validates its mechanical world picture is itself mechanistic, minimal and manipulative. In a word, it is the image of *mass man*— of man as the passive creature of ulterior forces working through and upon him, either from without (stimulus-response psychologies) or from within (instinct and drive psychologies). The image of mass man is so deeply ingrained, so neatly synchronized with the imperatives of the modern industrial state, that it has remained largely an unchallenged and inarticulate assumption both in the public mind and in the behavioural sciences (the true 'image makers' for the knowledge society). Thus the late C. Wright Mills, a radically dissenting sociologist, found it only natural under the conditions of mass technology that:[4]

> there should arise a conception of public opinion as a mere reaction—we cannot say 'response'—to the content of the mass media. In this view, the public is merely the collectivity of individuals each rather passively exposed to the mass media and rather helplessly opened up to the suggestions and manipulations that flow from these media.[4]

The behaviourist view of man as a helpless pawn in the fell clutch of circumstance is paralleled in its anti-Humanism by the recurrently popular doctrine which traces human conduct to blind instinctive urges, notably that of aggression, arising from a primordial and predatory ancestry. From social Darwinists through classical Freudians to the new school of ethological determinists led by Konrad Lorenz,[5] the instinctive theory of aggression has served to reinforce a fashionable pessimism concerning the human potential for rationality, responsibility and resourcefulness. The extraordinary acclamation which has been accorded this viewpoint in recent years (not, to be sure, among life-scientists, most of whom

---

[3] Mumford (1970), *op. cit.*
[4] Mills, C. Wright (1956), *The Power Elite*, New York: Oxford University Press, p. 305.
[5] Lorenz, Konrad (1966), *On Aggression*, New York: Harcourt, Brace and World.

repudiate it, but among the literary intelligentsia and the reading public) suggests the emergence of an intellectual and cultural backlash which expresses a desire for externally imposed constraint, discipline and authority—the theoretical correlates of law and order. To the widespread 'distrust of reason' which Reinhard Bendix discerned among the social sciences a score of years ago must now be added the distrust of man himself—the inclination to see him only as the victim or the villain, never as the victor, in his personal drama of existence.

Any adequate redefinition of Humanism must begin here, at the root metaphor. 'Modern man', as Norman Cousins pointed out a generation ago, is obsolete—whether in the form of Mass Man (the extension of the media), Economic Man (the product of the felicific calculus) or Organization Man (the creature of the lonely crowd). Surveying the dismal scene of behavioural science and human engineering at the end of the fifties, Mills declared: 'It is no wonder that the ideal of individuality has become moot: in our time, what is at issue is the very nature of man, the image we have of his limits and possibilities as man'.[6] The issue is still in doubt; nor can that existential choice of alternative selves be delegated to the experts, whose councils are sorely divided and whose authority to judge is in any case hotly disputed. (Who can forget the final warning of President Eisenhower against the 'danger that public policy could itself become the captive of a scientific-technological élite'?)

It may be, of course, as futurologists such as Zbigniew Brzezinsky[7] insist, that the hour of decision has already passed and the destiny of man has been ordained as that of a functional rôle-player in a technetronic society. On the other hand it may be, as prophets of the counterculture such as Charles Reich[8] tell us just as insistently, that a revolution in consciousness is already underway and that our laws, institutions and social structure are being transformed beneath our noses 'with amazing rapidity'. In either of these hypothetical cases, the necessity for individual choice and action—other than boarding the bandwagon or riding the juggernaut—would seem to be precluded.

[6] Mills, C. Wright (1959), *The Sociological Imagination*, New York: Oxford University Press.

[7] Brzezinsky, Zbigniew (1968), 'America in the Technetronic Age' in *Encounter*, vol. 30 (January 1968), pp. 16–26.

[8] Reich (1970), op. cit.

It may be, however, that another option exists—the option suggested by Mills of choosing between clearly competitive images of man, on the basis of a faith that man may choose himself and that his choice takes on the attributes of a self-fulfilling prophecy. If further guidance is needed in the act of definition and decision, I submit the recommendation of a great contemporary Humanist, Lewis Mumford:

> Not the Power Man, not the Profit Man, not the Mechanical Man, but the Whole Man, Man in Person, so to say, must be the central actor in the new drama of civilization . . . If technics is not to play a wholly destructive part in the future of Western Civilization we must now ask ourselves, for the first time, what sort of society and what kind of man are we seeking to produce?[9]

[9] Mumford, Lewis (1954), *In the Name of Sanity*, New York: Harcourt, Brace and World.

18

Humanism
and Behaviourism

B. F. SKINNER

THERE SEEM TO be two ways of knowing, or knowing about, another person. One is associated with existentialism, phenomenology and structuralism. It is a matter of knowing what a person is or what he is like or what he is coming to be or becoming. We try to know another person in this sense as we know ourselves. We share his feelings through sympathy or empathy. Through intuition we discover his attitudes, intentions and other states of mind. We communicate with him in the etymological sense of making ideas and feelings common to both of us. We do so more effectively if we have established good *interpersonal* relations. This is a passive, contemplative kind of knowing: if we want to predict what a person does or is likely to do, we assume that he, like us, will behave according to what he is; his behaviour, like ours, will be an expression of his feelings, states of mind, intentions, attitudes and so on.

The other way of knowing is a matter of what a person *does*. We can usually observe this as directly as any other phenomenon in the world; no special kind of knowing is needed. We explain why a person behaves as he does by turning to the environment rather than to inner states or activities. The environment was effective during the evolution of the species and we call its result on man the human genetic endowment. A member of the species is exposed to another part of that environment during his lifetime, and from it he acquires a repertoire of behaviour which converts an organism with a genetic endowment into a person. By analyzing these effects of the environment, we move toward the prediction and control of behaviour.

But can this formulation of what a person *does* neglect any available information about what he *is*? There are gaps in time and space between behaviour and the environmental events to which it is attributed and it is natural to try to fill them with an account of the intervening state of the organism. We do this when we summarize a long evolutionary history by speaking of genetic endowment. Should we not do the same for a personal history? An omniscient physiologist should be able to tell us, for example, how a person is changed when a bit of his behaviour is reinforced, and what he thus becomes should explain why he subsequently behaves in a different way. We argue in such a manner, for example, with respect to immunization. We begin with the fact that vaccination makes it less likely that a person will contract a disease at a later date. We say that he becomes immune and we speak of a state of immunity, which we then proceed to examine. An omniscient physiologist should be able to do the same for comparable states in the field of behaviour. He should also be able to change behaviour by changing the organism directly rather than by changing the environment. Is the existentialist, phenomenologist or structuralist not directing his attention precisely to such a mediating state?

A thoroughgoing dualist would say no, because for him what a person observes through introspection and what a physiologist observes with his special techniques are in different universes. But it is a reasonable view that what we feel when we have feelings are states of our own bodies and that the states of mind we perceive through introspection are other varieties of the same kinds of things. Can we not, therefore, anticipate the appearance of an omniscient physiologist and explore the gap between environment and behaviour by becoming more keenly aware of what we are?

It is at this point that a behaviouristic analysis of self-knowledge becomes most important and, unfortunately, is most likely to be misunderstood. Each of us possesses a small part of the universe within his own skin. It is not for that reason different from the rest of the universe, but it is a private possession: we have ways of knowing about it that are denied to others. It is a mistake, however, to conclude that the intimacy we thus enjoy means a special kind of understanding. We are, of course, stimulated directly by our own bodies. The so-called interoceptive nervous system responds to conditions important in deprivation and emotion. The proprioceptive system is involved in posture and movement and without it we could scarcely behave in a coordinated way. These two systems, together with the exteroceptive nervous system, are essential to effective behaviour. But knowing is more than responding to stimuli. A child responds to the colours of things before he 'knows his colours'. Knowing requires special contingencies of reinforcement that must be arranged by other people, and the contingencies involving private events are never very precise because other people are not effectively in contact with them. In spite of the intimacy of our own bodies, we know them less accurately than we know the world around us. And there are, of course, other reasons why we know the private world of others even less precisely.

The important issue, however, is not precision but subject matter. Just what can be known when we 'know ourselves'? The three nervous systems just mentioned have evolved under practical contingencies of survival, most of them nonsocial. (Social contingencies important for survival must have arisen in such fields as sexual and maternal behaviour.) They were presumably the only systems available when people began to 'know themselves' as the result of answering questions about their behaviour. In answering such questions as 'Do you see that?' or 'Did you hear that?' or 'What is that?' a person learns to observe his own responses to stimuli. In answering such questions as 'Are you hungry?' or 'Are you afraid?' he learns to observe states of his body related to deprivation and emotional arousal. In answering such questions as 'Are you going?' or 'Do you intend to go?' or 'Do you feel like going?' or 'Are you inclined to go?' he learns to observe the strength or probability of his behaviour. The verbal community asks such questions because the answers are important to it, and in a sense it thus makes the answers important to the person himself. The important fact is that such contingencies, social or nonsocial, involve nothing more than stimuli or responses; they do not involve mediating processes. We cannot fill the gap between behaviour and the environment of which it is a function through introspection because, to put the matter in crude physiological terms, we do not have nerves going to the right places. We cannot observe the states and events to which an omniscient physiologist would have access. What we feel when we have feelings and what we observe through introspection are nothing more than a rather miscellaneous set of

100

collateral products or by-products of the environmental conditions to which behaviour is related. (We do not act because we feel like acting, for example; we act *and* feel like acting for a common reason to be sought in our environmental history.) Do I mean to say that Plato never discovered the mind? Or that Aquinas, Descartes, Locke and Kant were preoccupied with incidental, often irrelevant by-products of human behaviour? Or that the mental laws of physiological psychologists like Wundt, the stream of consciousness of William James or the mental apparatus of Sigmund Freud have no useful place in the understanding of human behaviour? Yes, I do. And I put the matter strongly because, if we are to solve the problems that face us in the world today, this concern for mental life must no longer divert our attention from the environmental conditions of which human behaviour is a function.

But why have we attached so much importance to our feelings and states of mind, to the neglect of the environment? The answer seems to lie in the immediacy and the saliency of the stimuli. Many relevant events in our personal history pass without notice. For one thing, the behaviour to which they will eventually prove relevant has not yet occurred and cannot contribute to contingencies that would lead us to notice them. And if we have noticed them, we may quickly forget. But our feelings, 'ideas', 'felt intentions' and so on often overlap the behaviour to which they seem related, and they usually occur in just the place that would be occupied by a cause (on the principle of *post hoc, ergo propter hoc*). For example, we often feel a state of deprivation or emotion before we act in an appropriate way. If we say something to ourselves before saying it aloud, what we say aloud seems to be the expression of an inner thought. And if we say something aloud without first saying it to ourselves, it is tempting to suppose that we must be expressing a nonverbal thought.

This apparent causality lodged within the private world within a skin, together with the organization imposed upon it by the fact that all its determining conditions have occurred in the history of one person, generates a 'sense of self'. We feel there is an 'I' who knows what he is going to do and does it. Each of us is aware or conscious of at least one such self, which we learn to manage more or less effectively.

Since the only selves we know are human selves, it is often said that man is distinguished from other species precisely because he is

101

aware of himself and participates in the determination of his future. What distinguishes the human species, however, is the development of a culture, a social environment that contains the contingencies generating self-knowledge and self-control. It is this environment that has been so long neglected by those who have been concerned with the inner determination of conduct. The neglect has meant that better practices for building self-knowledge and self-management have been missed.

It is often said that a behaviouristic analysis 'dehumanizes man'. But it merely dispenses with a harmful explanatory fiction. In doing so it moves much more directly toward the goals that fiction was designed, erroneously, to serve. People understand themselves and manage themselves much more effectively when they understand the relevant contingencies.

Important processes in self-management lie in the fields of ethics and morals, where conflicts between immediate and deferred consequences are considered. One of the great achievements of a culture has been to bring remote consequences to bear upon the behaviour of the individual. We may design a culture in which the same results will be achieved much more efficiently by shifting our attention from ethical problem-solving or moral struggle to the external contingencies.

We may move from an inner agent to environmental determinants without neglecting the question of values. It has been argued that behaviourism is or pretends to be value free, but that no value-free science can properly deal with man *qua* man. What is wrong in the traditional argument can be seen in the expression 'value judgment'. An inner initiating agent is to *judge* things as good or bad. But a much more effective source of values is to be found in the environmental contingencies. The things people call good are positive reinforcers and they reinforce because of the contingencies of survival under which the species has evolved. Until recently, the species could survive famine, pestilence and other catastrophes only if its members procreated at every opportunity, and under such contingencies sexual contact became highly reinforcing. Sex is not reinforcing because it feels good; it is reinforcing *and* feels good for a common phylogenic reason. Some reinforcers may acquire their power during the life of the individual. Social goods, such as attention or approval, are created and used to induce people to behave in ways that are reinforcing to those who use them. The result may be good for the individual as well as for others, particularly when deferred consequences are mediated.

The values affecting those who are in charge of other people supply good examples of the importance of turning from the supposed attributes of an inner man to the contingencies affecting behaviour. There are five classical types of human beings who have been mistreated: the young, the elderly, prisoners, psychotics and retardates. Are they mistreated because those who are in charge of them lack sympathy, compassion or benevolence, or have no conscience? No, the important fact is that they are unable to retaliate. It is easy to mistreat any one of these five kinds of people without being mistreated in turn. It is important to make it clear that the *sources* of conscience are not to be found in psychological realities but in punitive sanctions.

An environmental analysis has a special advantage in promoting a kind of value concerned with the good of the culture. Cultures evolve under special contingencies of survival. A practice that makes a culture more likely to survive survives with the culture. Cultures become more successful in meeting contingencies of survival as they induce their members to behave in more and more subtle and complex ways. (Progress is not inevitable, of course, for there are extinct cultures as well as extinct species.) An important stage is reached when a culture induces some of its members to be concerned for its survival, because they may then design more effective practices.

Over the years, men and women have slowly and erratically constructed physical and social environments in which they have come closer to fulfilling or actualizing their potential. They have not changed themselves (that is a genetic problem which has not yet been solved); they have changed the world in which they live. In the design of his own culture, man could thus be said to control his destiny.

I would define a Humanist as one of those who, because of the environment to which he has been exposed, is concerned for the future of mankind. A movement that calls itself humanistic psychology takes a rather different line. It has been described as 'a third force' to distinguish it from behaviourism and psychoanalysis; but 'third' should not be taken to mean advanced, nor should 'force' suggest power. Since behaviourism and psychoanalysis both view human behaviour as a determined system, humanistic psychologists have emphasized a contrast by defending the autonomy of the

103

individual. They have insisted that a person can transcend his environment, that he is more than a causal stage between behaviour and environment, that he determines what environmental forces will act upon him—in a word, that he has free choice. The position is most at home in existentialism, phenomenology and structuralism, because the emphasis is on what a person is or is becoming. Maslow's expression 'self-actualization' sums it up nicely: the individual is to fulfil himself—not merely through gratification, of course, but through 'spiritual growth'.

Humanistic psychologists are not unconcerned about the good of others or even the good of a culture or of mankind, but such a formulation is basically selfish. Its development can be traced in the struggle for political, religious and economic freedom, where a despotic ruler could be overthrown only by convincing the individual that he was the source of the power used to control him. The strategy has had beneficial results, but it has led to an excessive aggrandizement of the individual, which may lead in turn either to new forms of tyranny or to chaos. The supposed right of the individual to acquire unlimited wealth which he is free to use as he pleases often results in a kind of despotism; the Hindu concern for personal growth in spirituality has been accompanied by an almost total neglect of the social environment.

Better forms of government are not to be found in better rulers, better educational practices in better teachers, better economic systems in more enlightened management, or better therapy in more compassionate therapists. Neither are they to be found in better citizens, students, workers or patients. The age-old mistake is to look for salvation in the character of autonomous men and women rather than in the social environments that have appeared in the evolution of cultures and that can now be explicitly designed.

But turning from man *qua* man to the external conditions of which man's behaviour is a function, it has been possible to design better practices in the care of psychotics and retardates, in child care, in education (in both contingency management in the classroom and the design of instructional material), in incentive systems in industry and in penal institutions. In these and many other areas we can now work more effectively for the good of the individual, for the greatest good of the greatest number and for the good of the culture or of mankind as a whole. These are certainly humanistic concerns and no one who calls himself a Humanist can afford to neglect them. Men and women have never faced a greater threat to the future of their species. There is much to be done and done quickly, and nothing less than the active prosecution of a science of behaviour will suffice.

19
Behaviourism
is a Humanism
KENNETH MACCORQUODALE

BEHAVIOURISM IS SIMPLY the application of the methods of experimental science to the behaviour of organisms, an application that was inevitable once the tremendous power of these methods became evident in the explanation and ordering of physical, chemical, astronomical and nonbehavioural puzzles. The methods of science give us decision rules for distinguishing between fact and convenient fiction in nature, especially insofar as we are concerned with causality. This characteristic commends the methods of scientific observation and reasoning to the student of behaviour, whose subject matter is, by long heritage, overridden with curiosity-assuaging but utterly untestable lore. To forbid the application of science to the facts of behaviour will have to be done by fiat, not reason. Because the voice of science is itself impeccably rational, insistently reasonable and forever self-correcting, it cannot be deduced out of existence. Science may be unwelcome in the domain of human behaviour but it is reasonable all the same.

Forbidding by fiat may, of course, be based upon an understandable first-blush feeling that it is somehow bad form, dehumanizing and disrespectful to man to look for him in the orderly, deterministic universe of other things in nature—or to speak of any man-in-person as an instance of man-in-general. But the rationality and origins of man's discomfort are somewhat puzzling. Simply looking at a man, especially with the detachment and distance of science, and reporting only what can be seen, does not alter him in any way. It does not detract from his essence, nor deny his uniqueness, nor destroy his integrity. The scientist cannot place man's behaviour securely within the natural order—he can only look for it there. Man's distaste at finding himself so located is probably something he will simply have to get used to, since it seems unlikely that he can talk his way out of it. In light of this, it is interesting that the timing of the renaissance of the third revolution of psychology coincides nicely with the rise of an impressively effective behaviourist alternative. Anguish and rage at *Walden Two*[1] have been predicated on a respectful (and justified) suspicion that the principles that were to run this utopia, including operant conditioning, would indeed work—and that someone might just do it. The true disbeliever, however, would greet the attempt with glee, not fear, confidently anticipating its *coup de grâce*.

When science discovers and enumerates the variables that control man's behaviour, man does not lose his autonomy and freedom; at worst, he discovers that they had unsuspected limits. Yet he loses nothing he once had. The limits are those imposed by the laws of nature, not the laws of scientists. No scientist can actually create control, he can only reveal it.

Even so, behaviourism is not a doctrine of man's helplessness in a deterministic world. Quite the contrary, once the variables that affect behaviour are firmly identified in scientific laws, man is free at last to alter his fate—the course of his history, mind you, not his inner essence—by, literally, exercising control in manipulating the variables that are already affecting his behaviour for better or for worse. He does not choose behaviour directly, nor does he tinker with the machine. He controls the input, arranging for some inputs to occur and preventing others. He is free to choose rationally and effectively, just as Dostoyevsky's underground man, seemingly a realist and a good behaviourist, chose to stick his tongue out—but only on the sly! On sober second thought, the underground man sided with Thomas Huxley after all; neither of them favoured outright caprice and randomness of choice.

One apparent consequence of applying the methods of science to man's behaviour is that such an application analytically disassembles the behaviour and seems to destroy or ignore man's wholeness or self in doing so. In actual practice, however, although the behaviourist does indeed analyze, he does not leave man in pieces. He analyzes in order to discover and conceptualize the components and origins of behaviour as an organized whole. Selves—as detached, unique, whole essences—are not, on the other hand, susceptible to scientific analysis and therefore require that some other method of inquiry be applied by scholars with other goals.

[1] Skinner, B. F. (1962), *Walden Two*, New York: Collier Macmillan.

Above all, behaviourism is not really a bleak conspiracy to delimit man's choice and freedom by artificial constraint, any more than physics is a conspiracy against atoms. When poor, belaboured Watson said he wanted to 'control man's reactions', he was proposing not to apply psychology against man, but only to test the accuracy of his science. He did not want to make beggars and thieves; he wanted to see if it could be done. The decision to apply science, for or against, is not a scientific one, nor is it a part of the science applied. This is surely elementary and needs no further argument.

The variables that affect behaviour, if left uncontrolled, may work mischievously and cruelly against man. The true authoritarian personality is the one who says: 'Don't teach, don't touch, don't tinker. Let man choose, badly and stupidly and in ignorance, and live miserably. He is so gloriously free to do so. Let him.' The question is, is man free *not* to do so? Behaviourism, by locating the means of self-control outside behaviour, where they are accessible and manageable, gives man this choice. That is hardly inhumane, and hardly disrespectful of man's dignity.

It is somewhat poignant and paradoxical then that the behavioural scientist, surely a 'human person', is exhorted, in the name of a doctrine that emphasizes freedom, choice and personal respect, to desist at once—especially since the behaviourist sees the product of his own inquiry contributing precisely to man's freedom, choice and self-respect. As a scientist, the behaviourist is himself in the humanistic traditions of inquiry, reason and understanding.

20
Scientific Humanism
ANTONY FLEW

I TAKE MY STAND as a scientific Humanist. There is a reason for employing both words together to describe this standpoint. This reason is not simply to win two moderately popular hooray-terms over onto my side; as was, I suspect, the case with the coinage 'Christian Science' introduced as a label for a doctrine which is certainly no more Christian than it is scientific. For as I construe the phrase scientific Humanist the first word indicates an approach to matters of fact while the second refers primarily to fundamental criteria of evaluation. To adopt such a scientific approach unreservedly is to accept as ultimate in all matters of fact and real existence the appeal to the evidence of experience alone; a court subordinate to no higher authority, to be overridden by no prejudice however comfortable. To commit oneself to Humanist values is to put the welfare of human beings first, to make people supremely important, to adopt human welfare and human goods as the ultimate criteria of right and wrong.

The first emphasis, therefore, in this consciously Humian statement is on the fundamental importance of distinguishing questions of fact from questions of value.[1] It may be perfectly consistent, albeit unfortunate or misguided, to be both Humanist and yet in some sense un- or anti-scientific, or to be rigorously scientific while indifferent to the claims of human welfare. It is indeed not hard today to find people who actualize, whether consistently or not, one or other of these alternative possibilities.

Next, it may be objected that at least the scientific half of the scientific Humanist commitment is emptily non-controversial. So in some areas and in some circles it is. In the field of physics, or of natural science generally, and in the circles in which most contribu-

[1] For a discussion within a Humian framework of the possibility and importance of such a distinction see W. D. Hudson (ed.) (1970), *The Is/Ought Question*, London: Macmillan, New York: St Martin's Press.

tors to the present volume move most of the time, the claims of a scientific approach are rarely contested. Yet even here we should not forget two recent challenges. For in 1950 in the Encyclical *Humani Generis*[2] the Vatican reiterated its traditional pretensions, once enforced against Galileo, to the authority to overrule the findings of scientific inquiry. 'In the present state of scientific and theological opinion, this question may be legitimately canvassed by research. . . . At the same time . . . there must be a readiness on all sides to accept the arbitrament of the Church, as being entrusted by Christ with the task of interpreting the Scriptures aright, and the duty of safeguarding the doctrines of the Faith.' The issue in question then and there was, unbelievably, the fact of the evolutionary origin of species.

Again, precisely the same issue was raised in a more deadly way in the affair of Academician Lysenko. For the heart of that matter was not whether or not the facts happened to be as Lysenko and his mighty backers said they were. It was, rather, whether the scientific appeal to evidence and to free inquiry should be overridden by the higher authority of the Marxist scriptures, as interpreted by the Central Committee of the Communist Party of the USSR and thereafter enforced with all the enormous power of the Soviet super-state.

But these two challenges constitute only rearguard actions. It is in other areas that we find the real obstacles to a scientific approach to matters of fact, in the territories of the human as opposed to the natural sciences. These obstacles can be at least as much internal as external. For it is here that our interests are most deeply, most directly and most widely engaged. We may, through some general ideological involvement, with Communism, with Catholicism or whatever, acquire a strong derived interest in making out that the facts of astronomy or biology are thus and thus, rather than so and so. But very properly, fortunately and understandably the facts in these cases lack—as the men of the media have it—immediate human interest. Equally properly and understandably—but in the present context unfortunately—we are also bound to have direct and underived desires to make out that certain facts about human nature or about social organization are so and so, rather than thus and thus. To offset such humanly natural bias, the social scientist

[2] Translated as *False Trends in Modern Teaching*, London: Catholic Truth Society, 1950.

needs to develop an overriding desire to know the facts whatever they may be; and he also needs to have institutions which will mobilize other, perhaps intrinsically less creditable, desires to press against the pressure of his biases.

It is for this obvious reason of inescapable human involvement that it is so much harder, and so much more personally demanding, to become a professional who truly merits the diploma title 'social scientist' than it is to become a good natural scientist; and that itself is, in all conscience, hard enough. Once these elementary considerations are properly appreciated one cannot but be appalled by the fact that in Britain the universities have in recent years expanded social studies, and above all departments of sociology, at a rate which would have been thought impossible for physics or mathematics. Again, once the need to counter biases is appreciated we should be shocked by the survey evidence of the overwhelmingly one sided political orientation of America's sociologists. For how can any sociologist hope to overcome his own unavoidably human biases if he is not constantly exposed to the informed professional criticism of others whose equally unavoidable wishes are opposed to his own?

Example after example could be produced of reluctance to discover relevant human and social facts or to recognize these facts when they have been discovered. For instance: for many years in Britain, writers in the most popular Sunday newspapers used to call for the reintroduction of judicial flogging, since supposedly 'it stood to reason' and 'all experience showed' that flogging must be the uniquely effective way to still a wave of violent crime. Yet these rabble-rousing writers never tried to come to terms with the coolly-marshalled evidence that this apparently most fitting punishment is in fact, in the cases for which it is popularly recommended, 'counter-productive'.[3]

Or again—just to prevent any growing smugness in Hampstead, or in Greenwich Village!—consider the ferocious reaction of the whole liberal establishment to Jensen's attempt actually to investigate the question of whether certain racial groups are on average superior or inferior to others in respect of their inherited capabilities. Since skin colour certainly is inherited, and since at least some differences of capacity are surely also hereditary, the suggestion that there may

[3] See the *Report of the Departmental Committee on Corporal Punishment*, London: HMSO, 1938.

be correlations can certainly not be dismissed out of hand as too implausible to merit investigation. Insofar as the great chorus of condemnation was a reaction, not to alleged and certainly remediable weaknesses in execution but to the heresy of attempting to put a dogma to the test of fact, this reaction revealed a refusal to accept the scientific part of the scientific Humanist commitment.

It surely revealed also a failure to appreciate the fundamental difference between facts and norms. For the belief 'that all men are created equal, and endowed with certain natural rights', is not to be construed as committing anyone to the dogma that all the babies—and particularly now the babies of different colours—come equal in capabilities. It is, rather, a belief about how the babies as they grow ought to be treated. There is, therefore, nothing inconsistent in maintaining that all men, regardless of all differences in capability, ought to be granted equal rights; nor yet in adding, as I should, that some incapacities—like blindness, for example—call for special help. (When Stalin responded to normative claims of human equality by insisting that he knew men to be unequal in their abilities, what he said was true but irrelevant.)

My third main point is that to commit oneself to Humanist values is to put the welfare of human beings first, to make people supremely important, to adopt their goods as the ultimate criteria of right and wrong. But by itself this is a very general commitment, mainly significant in what it rejects. It gets content only insofar as it is given some special filling.

Generally, such Humanism must be at least in theory fundamentally opposed to any religious ethic—notwithstanding that there may be great scope for practical co-operation between theists and Humanists. There must be fundamental opposition in theory because a religious ethic has to put God's will first. But this may still allow for practical harmony insofar as the believed content of that will happens to coincide with the norms of Humanism.

Specially, there is enormous room for disagreement about what is human and what constitutes welfare. For instance, as far as Marx—especially the young Marx—can be truly said to be committed to Humanist values, this involved, negatively, a rejection of all divine claims plus, positively, a devotion to the species man rather than to the flesh and blood individual human being. His diagnosis of that endemic evil alienation was thus achieved by an abstract analysis of man and labour, not by reference to individual

112

patients to ask of what, if anything, they themselves complain. It is, therefore, not altogether inappropriate that the concept of democracy espoused by those who claim today to be Marxists requires no reference to the actual desires of the people concerned as expressed in free elections. It is more a matter of the (Leninist) government doing what it thinks that the people need than of what they actually want. Of course, my wants and my needs may happen to coincide, and so may those of the people of the German Democratic Republic, even if the Red Army is always at hand to ensure that the question is never put to the test.

Fourth, it is worth pointing out that a commitment to Humanist values does not in any way presuppose starry-eyed illusions about the squalid realities of human inclinations and behaviour. It is perfectly proper and possible to insist on the supreme importance of human welfare without basing this evaluation on, or being committed to, any foolish doctrine of the original, present or even future virtue of all mankind. (The case is similar to that of constitutional democracy; though there it may be precisely your conviction that no men—not even far-off foreign men in Hanoi, Havana or Peking—are good enough to be entrusted with absolute power, which supports your demand for constitutional and electoral checks on all government.)

Fifth, not only are there various species within the general class of Humanist commitment, but those species themselves are not necessarily integrated and systematic. Certainly my own special commitment is not to a system of casuistry. Nor does it provide a talismanic touchstone for settling all questions of right and wrong. Rather it is a logically prior fundamental decision as to the sort of considerations to be taken as relevant to such questions. Welfare is not a simple homogeneous something which can be measurably maximized. One man's satisfaction may cost another man's frustration. One sort of good may be the enemy of another. Joy is incommensurable with misery; especially when one man's joy has to be balanced against another man's misery.

To make this commitment rarely is and never needs to be a solemn deliberate action marking a decisive turning point in life, a secular conversion. Many people nowadays have been Humanists all their lives without recognizing it, making and expressing their ultimate value commitments in every several action and inaction of their lives. Nor does it require that all accepted principles and loyalties be

113

called into question, and rejected or retained in the light of a deliberate assessment of their contribution to human welfare. Only that if and when such questions do arise, it should be in this light that they are judged. In morals as elsewhere, reformist conservatism rather than revolutionary utopianism is the rational constructive approach. It is safer and more sensible to continue in whatever ways we have been following, until and unless we find positive good reason to the contrary, rather than to attempt a radical reconstruction on a site first swept clear of every vestige of the past.[4]

[4] See Sir Karl Popper (1945), *The Open Society and its Enemies*, London: Routledge and Kegan Paul.

VII PERSONAL TESTAMENTS

21

Humanism as I View It

LESTER A. KIRKENDALL

M Y MOVEMENT INTO HUMANISM was a gradual one, not the consequence of a rebellion. Born and reared in a religiously fundamentalist community in western Kansas, I very early felt the inconsistencies of its approach to ordering my life. I found it filled with hypocrisies and full of confusing and contradictory statements. Those who followed the fundamentalist doctrine never seemed able to live up to what they thought was demanded of them, nor were they satisfied with what others did. While they preached adherence to a loving Father, some of them were so hostile and unloving as to make it apparent even to an unsophisticated boy that their allegiance meant nothing significant to them.

What I saw early in individual lives I later saw in our national life—namely, the spectacle of the so-called 'greatest Christian nation on earth' making the most unabashed and open warfare against other nations and all too often spending its resources on hostile attacks upon its neighbours, rather than reaching out in peace and love. Consequently I was never allied with the fundamentalists, although I still felt, probably through cultural pressures, the need for some kind of religious affiliation.

During my high school days I joined the Methodist Church. I worked for a number of years within that organization, and in the meantime married the minister's daughter. Even here I found the same contradictions and hypocrisies in individual lives, perhaps somewhat less obviously displayed than was the case in the fundamentalist community. Later, as a university teacher, I became associated with the Unitarian Fellowship where I found a more congenial home.

Throughout all this time I was becoming more and more convinced that there is no supernatural power possessing the ability to reward one for good deeds or to punish one for disobedience to the

117

command of a Deity. Indeed, 'good deeds' gradually came to seem more and more parochial, and more and more determined by mores and social custom. The faith demanded by traditional religion seemed a blind one rooted in nothing that a searching intelligence could respect. More and more I perceived that man himself had to be the focus of concern. Either man would save himself, or he would not be saved. He had altered his environment, had made his own problems, created his great moments, and all these were his own responsibility. His pressing problems had to be solved by man, or they would not be solved. It is only through a knowledge of man, his strengths and weaknesses, his capacities and potentialities, his ability to challenge the best that is within him, that we can hope for a better world. This is my philosophy, and it is in this sense that I am a Humanist for I think this point of view is central to Humanism. I might add also that I regard Humanism essentially as a philosophy of man, his needs and his potentialities. I do not see it as a religion in the traditional sense.

This philosophy calls for the greatest possible awareness of man, for only as we understand ourselves and our capabilities can we work successfully with our problems and realize our full potentialities. In short, faith is required, but an informed faith based on an increasing knowledge of man. There is much yet to be learned about human nature, but the weight of evidence makes it clear that while man is a complex being he is essentially a social animal.

One may well ask: why, if man is a social animal, has he made such a botch of his group relationships? Why is there so much strife, racial prejudice and warfare? The answer is very complex and in many respects unclear. Much of the problem lies in the limited scope of knowledge that most people have of mankind in general and in the powerful nature of the aggressive impulse, which is also a part of man's character and one which he has yet to learn how to direct wisely. Man's intense curiosity and his desire to explore every aspect of his environment also places him in many difficult situations.

Yet, all these complexities notwithstanding, I agree with Erich Fromm, Carl Rogers, Abraham Maslow, Ashley Montagu and others when they say that man can find satisfaction only through his sociality. In fact, his very survival depends upon his finding satisfying relationships with others. The imperative need, the behavioural scientists say, is for men to associate with and relate to each other. This basic need is behind the whole gamut of intimate human

118

relations that man seeks—behind what we call love, in the broadest sense of the word. This point of view I share.

From this tenet there follow several corollaries. First, I am interested in Humanism because, if it is viable, it must include all humankind. How odd, how parochial to set oneself off as 100 per cent American, 100 per cent Chinese or 100 per cent Russian when our greatest need is for everyone to recognize his affiliation with all mankind! Those Vietnamese shot down in the massacre of My Lai were my brothers; their agony is my agony. Skin colour, hair texture, eye slant—these are inconsequential. Any meaningful Humanism must speak in a language that includes all mankind. Until it does that, it will be falling short of its goal.

Second, much stress is laid upon rational thinking and the intellectual processes underlining the development and success of Humanism. With this I agree, but only if we give adequate recognition to human emotional needs also. Man is a creature who needs to care and be cared for, to give and receive love. Thus Humanism must recognize man as a unity. His reason and his emotions are inseparably linked, and Humanists must take this into account.

Third, to me, the structures of social organization become secondary to the needs of individuals. We have the habit of making sacrosanct many social structures that at one time served a very necessary and significant purpose. Because the structures have existed relatively unchanged for so long, we assume they must remain unchanged. Yet never at any time in the past have family, marriage or sexual patterns—or patterns of any kind, for that matter —been uniform throughout the world. We cannot expect them to be so now. Varying historical patterns, differing cultural demands and inevitable future changes mean that the structures of today will not serve tomorrow and ought not to be expected to. It is the task of Humanism to assess and evaluate these structures and to help develop those family, marriage, sexual, industrial, legal and nationalistic patterns that will best enable human beings to realize their potentialities.

Fourth, our culture has always strongly advocated the right of the individual to realize the fullest achievement of his capacities. This is as it should be, yet it is easy to forget that the individual is inseparably linked to the group for his personal satisfaction. As Maslow puts it, 'good human beings will generally need a good society in which to grow . . . [this is necessary if they are] to actualize themselves as good specimens.' It is impossible therefore to consider the individual apart from his group and the broad society. The demands of the individual and the needs of the group can never be fully harmonized, but their inseparability must not be forgotten.

Such issues raise many perplexing problems, some of which, because of our advanced stage of technological development, may even now be unsolvable. Biological research that contemplates genetic engineering, restrictive breeding through selected sperm and ova, the development of the foetus outside the uterus, 'host mothers', the determination of the sex of the child—all these and other prospects—raise both tremendously exciting and at the same time dangerous problems for mankind.

The increasing separation of man from nature is yet another issue. Man has come to consider himself beyond nature, and the Biblical injunction to 'subdue' the earth has been taken so literally that further pursuit of this objective may well see his extinction. Man must not forget that he is a part of nature and that nature is within him—and neither must the Humanist forget. One of the ethical tasks of Humanism is to weigh and evaluate the way in which man's developments impinge upon nature.

These considerations, then, suggest why I am a Humanist and something of what I think our present circumstances mean for Humanism. The humanistic contribution lies not only in helping man solve his present and forthcoming problems, but in insuring a better, more humane world for those who follow us. The demands facing Humanism represent challenge enough for any daring soul.

22

Humanism as Activity

ROY P. FAIRFIELD

HUMANISM IS A PHILOSOPHY which must be defined by action as well as logic and words. Hence humanism is:

. . . a man and woman standing in awe of the aurora borealis or with creative delight in the glow of having made a cake, a chair or a garden

. . . a woman labouring with strength and dignity to deliver a child

. . . an Aeschylus or a Robinson Jeffers perched on a rocky crag peering over the Aegean or Pacific and composing verse to describe man's relationship with the sun, the sea, the stars, the birds, the razor grasses

. . . a Freud, Fromm or Jung penetrating the inner universes of man's mind, consciousness or configurations of sparking synapses to discover man's relationship to himself

. . . two children exploring their genitals or playing with a garter snake to see what makes it move, reflecting that curiosity of which 'growing up' seems almost inevitably to deprive them

. . . an empathetic glance across a room, one signalling 'Fear not, for I am with you', a glance calming the seas of anxiety

. . . a gentle touch on a mourning shoulder upon the death of a friend or relative

. . . a caring which manifests itself in travelling the tenth mile, not merely the second

. . . the sensitivity reading 'Help!' into the language of a letter, reading between the words as well as the lines of a message

. . . a courageous listening while a friend, counsellor or neighbour talks his or her way toward clarification of a personal problem

. . . an understanding 'Hello' in the middle of the night when another person, feeling a deep need for human contact, phones to break the silence of slumber

121

. . . a perception of need to change oneself in order to escape technological destruction, bureaucratic anonymity or crippling socialization; a perception and a plan of action to develop and implement strategies for self-change, and a faith that such a plan is workable

. . . an attitude of openness toward the love, the strengths and even the foibles of particular persons (not mere abstractions) of other cultures, subcultures, races, creeds, clans and viewpoints; an eager willingness to engage in dialogue and feeling toward such other-humans who are *not* subhuman, inhuman or nonhuman *because of* their differentness

. . . an enthusiasm for getting up in the morning to see what one may learn from other humans

. . . an acceptance of the fact that each human is the measure of all things and that this measure is complex, is unique, is mystical (in the nonreligious sense), is worthy of human and humane analyses, is multidimensional and hence to be observed and appreciated from both *gestalt* and linear perspectives

. . . a willingness to try to write a haiku or master a tea ceremony to get a feel for a Japanese angle of vision . . . or to build an igloo to gain a better sense of the Eskimo

. . . the cultivation of a taste for *tasting* French pastry, Greek souflakia, Indian curry, West African chop, Dutch rijsttafel, Mexican enchiladas, Black soul food

. . . the joy in matching wits with a peerless punster or famous logician, either in person or through works of art

. . . the strength of jetting an ocean to revisit a friend or an Old Master's painting or a view of the Acropolis

. . . the basking in the memory of one's emotional state in seeing a piece of sculpture such as 'Nike Tying Her Sandal', a tear burning its way down a friend's cheek, a one-hour deep ochre sunset while flying from Spain to Puerto Rico

. . . the tingling sensation ('chills down my back') of the memory of one's first ski ride down a new slalom course, a first lover's kiss, a first reading of Whitman's *Leaves of Grass*, Shakespeare's *Romeo & Juliet* or Aldous Huxley's *Brave New World*

. . . the sense of wonder in staring upwards at the Empire State Building or Michelangelo's dome on St Peter's, staring outward from Mt Fujiyama, staring downward at an iceberg from a jet off the coast of Greenland

. . . the deep satisfaction of hearing a simple 'Well done!' from a respected person, the solution of a complex mathematical or social problem, the climbing of a mountain ('because it's there'), the identification with a team which has won a hard game or even lost it with dignity and courage

. . . the tears which flow when one hears the *Chorale* of Beethoven's *Ninth Symphony* if one recalls that Beethoven was stone deaf when he wrote it . . . symbolizing man's ability to triumph over incredible physical handicaps . . . or tears which come from listening to a popular song touching a romantic nerve . . . or tears while watching helplessly as a friend dies from cancer, but dies nobly

. . . tears, both male and female.

In short, man lives humanly when he dares let himself be human in *every* dimension of his being, in a *gestalt* including the rawest emotion as well as the profoundest rationality. And both the rawness and profundity can be frightening because they can lead to insensitivity as well as beauty, to destruction of oneself as well as others, to a Hitler as well as an Erasmus. The Humanist-in-action will recognize the need for humour (lest he take his cosmic situation and presence too seriously), the need for accepting paradox (to be of use, one must take abuse; the closer one gets to achieving social and political power, the less power one has to maintain one's total humanness), the imperative of relating to irony (no man ever *is* what he may seem to be) and the urgency of expressing oneself somehow, so that one's outer manifestations sculpt the clay of one's inner identity. And clay it is, too, malleable and moist, shapeable into countless configurations . . . clay and verve mixed generously.

23
Humanism:
a Joyous View
LLOYD AND MARY MORAIN

H UMANISM IS REMARKABLY APPROPRIATE for today, reinforcing positive aspects of modern thinking and providing alternative sources of strength where older ideas no longer seem relevant. A wide spectrum of people around the world are coming to recognize that personal relationships within and between classes, sexes and national and ethnic groups are not eternally fixed. There is growing awareness that deeds can be more important than creeds, acts more important than words. Yet many people feel the need for something more—some point of view from which to order their actions and their world, something to take the place of the traditional guideposts for personal and social behaviour now crumbling at an accelerated rate. With increasing knowledge it has seemed more difficult to tie accepted thought and behaviour to unaltering cosmic and cultural laws.

Humanistic philosophy is the result of many influences and forces, and is necessarily described in general terms. Men and women with varied life experiences are attracted to Humanism for different reasons and 'read' it in different ways. For some it is a psychology of self-actualization, for others a naturalistic philosophy or religion, for still others a way of life.

Many Humanists find a special relevance in a picture of *homo sapiens* within nature. Let us see what could be developed from this particular angle which might help, and even inspire, a seeker for order and meaning in this world of the present. There are positive intellectual excitements open to the person who wholeheartedly accepts the idea that humankind is entirely within nature, boasting no supernatural aspects. Here we are, with all our complexities, creativities and self-consciousness, alone in the midst of very much simpler forces and simpler living creatures,

124

and to a varying extent at the mercy of these forces and creatures. Here we are, evolved through uncounted ages from the interreaction of chemicals and energies. Is this not the most awe-inspiring, downright spine-tingling drama that can be conceived?

Unlike other living things, human beings can experience directly while at the same time understanding that such experience comes about because of processes in great part hidden. We can enjoy a sunset even while vaguely knowing that this riot of colour comes from light rays and particles in the air. Humanists are often peculiarly able to enjoy this 'double vision'. Most of them thrive on explanation—physiological, chemical or any other plausible sort. Any system that restricts attention to direct sensory or subjective experience robs life of this type of richness, this human multi-dimensionality. Seen in these terms, science is not only a purveyor of easier, safer life for the layman, but also helps to enrich knowledge and insight.

Human beings are unique in their experience of nature, yet deeply a part of it, as much a part as the chipmunk or the lofty redwood. Humanists savour and take joy from this paradox. We can feel a closeness with other living things because we have thrown overboard special pretensions and privileges. We are willing to face with all that lives the tragedies and mysteries of life and death. We can feel ourselves children of the earth, recognizing that our entire history is bounded by it.

From these thoughts and feelings springs a sense of kinship with all humans, brothers and sisters in this strange human situation, similar in needs and aspirations however varied in social custom. Those Humanists who follow this route come, in their own way, to the basic ideas at the heart of the philosophy—the value of the individual and concern for his welfare and the welfare of the race as a whole.

Humanism is a philosophy of change, preparing one for change, encouraging the interested acceptance of changes. Asserting from all approaches the value of the human adventure, this philosophy is able to give some sense of order, purpose and inspiration.

VIII VARIETIES OF HUMANISM ON THE WORLD SCENE

24
Naturalistic Humanism

CORLISS LAMONT

UMANISM IS SUCH A WARM and attractive word that in the twentieth century it has been adopted by various groups, often diametrically opposed in ideology. Some usages of this term are most questionable. For instance, the Catholics, who still adhere to many outworn myths of Christian supernaturalism, promote what they call Catholic Humanism; while the Communists, who reject in practice political democracy and civil liberties, continually talk of socialist Humanism. But the Humanism that has become increasingly influential in this century, in English-speaking countries and throughout the non-Communist world, is naturalistic Humanism. This is the Humanism that I have supported through the written and spoken word for some forty years.

To define naturalistic Humanism in a nutshell; it rejects all forms of supernaturalism, pantheism and metaphysical idealism; it considers man's supreme ethical aim as working for the welfare of all humanity in this one and only life, using the methods of reason, science and democracy for the solution of problems.

To become more specific, I shall enumerate the chief elements in my understanding of Humanism.

First, Humanism believes that nature or the universe makes up the totality of existence and is completely self-operating according to natural law, with no need for a God or gods to keep it functioning. This cosmos, unbounded in space and infinite in time, consists fundamentally of a constantly changing system of matter and energy, and is neutral in regard to man's well-being and values.

Second, Humanism holds that the race of man is the present culmination of a time-defying evolutionary process on this planet that has lasted billions of years; that man exists as an inseparable unity of mind and body, and that therefore after death there can be no personal immortality or survival of consciousness.

Third, in working out its basic views on man and the universe,

E

129

Humanism relies on reason, and especially on the established facts, laws and methods of modern experimental science. In general, men's best hope for solving their problems is through the use of intelligence and scientific method applied with vision and determination. Courage, love and perseverance provide emotional drive for successfully coping with difficulties, but it is reason that finds the actual solution. Science and technology are to be considered instruments for the service of mankind and must always be controlled in the light of ecological, ethical, economic and other values.

Fourth, Humanism is opposed to all theories of universal determinism, fatalism or predestination and believes that human beings possess genuine freedom of choice (free will) in making decisions both important and unimportant. Free choice is conditioned by inheritance, education, health, the external environment (including economic conditions) and other factors. Nonetheless, it remains real and substantial. Humanism rejects alike Christian theistic determinism, Marxist economic determinism and the determinism of the behaviourist psychologists. It places on the human individual full responsibility for his decisions and actions.

Fifth, Humanism advocates an ethics or morality that grounds all human values in this-earthly experiences and relationships, and that views man as a functioning unity of physical, emotional and intellectual faculties. The Humanist holds as his highest ethical goal the this-worldly happiness, freedom and progress—economic, cultural and material—of all mankind, irrespective of nation, race, religion, sex or economic status. Reserving the word 'love' for his family and friends, he has an attitude of compassionate concern toward his fellow men in general.

Sixth, in the controversial realm of sex relations, Humanism entirely rejects dualistic theories that separate soul from body and claim that the highest morality is to keep the soul pure and undefiled from physical pleasure and desire. The Humanist regards sexual emotions and their fulfilment as healthy, beautiful and nature's wonderful way of making possible the continued reproduction of the human race. While Humanism advocates high standards of conduct between the sexes, it rejects the puritanism of the past and looks upon sex love and sex pleasure as among the greatest of human experiences and values.

Seventh, Humanism believes that the good life is best attained by an individual's combining the more personal satisfactions with significant work and other activities that contribute to the welfare of one's city, nation, university, trade union or other social unit. Worthwhile work is likely to make a person happier. At the same time everyone must exercise a considerable amount of self-interest, if only to keep alive and healthy. Normal and legitimate self-interest can be harmoniously united with ethical idealism and altruistic endeavours on behalf of the community.

Eighth, Humanism supports the widest possible development of the arts and the awareness of beauty, so that the aesthetic experience may become a pervasive reality in the life of man. The Humanist eschews the artificial distinction between the fine arts and the useful arts and asserts that the common objects of daily use should embody a fusion of utility and grace. The mass production of industrial goods by machinery need not necessarily defeat this aim. Among other things, and particularly in America, Humanism calls for the planned architectural reconstruction of towns and cities, so that beauty may prevail in our urban life. (In other countries, Humanism cries out against destructive reconstruction.)

Ninth, Humanism gives special emphasis to man's appreciation of the beauty and splendour of nature. The Humanist energetically backs the widespread efforts for conservation, the extension of park areas and the protection of wild life. Long before sound ecology and anti-pollution measures became widely accepted as national goals, he was campaigning for these very things. The Humanist's keen responsiveness to every sort of natural beauty evokes in him a feeling of profound kinship with nature and its myriad forms of life.

Tenth, for the actualization of human happiness and freedom everywhere on earth, Humanism advocates the establishment of international peace, democracy and a high standard of living throughout the world. Humanists, in their concern for the welfare of all nations, peoples and races, adopt William Lloyd Garrison's aphorism, 'Our country is the world; our countrymen are all mankind.' It follows that Humanists are strongly opposed to all forms of racial and nationalist prejudice. Humanism is international in spirit and scope, as evidenced by the activities of the International Humanist and Ethical Union.

Eleventh, Humanism believes that the best type of government

131

is some form of political democracy, which includes civil liberties and full freedom of expression throughout all areas of economic, political and cultural life. Reason and science are crippled unless they remain unfettered in the pursuit of truth. In the United States, the Humanist vigorously supports the democratic guarantees in the Bill of Rights and the Constitution.

Twelfth, Humanism, in accordance with scientific method, encourages the unending questioning of basic assumptions and convictions in every field of thought. This includes, of course, philosophy, naturalistic Humanism and the twelve points I have presented in this attempt at definition. Humanism is not a new dogma, but is a developing philosophy ever open to experimental testing, newly discovered facts and more rigorous reasoning.

I do not claim that every Humanist will accept all the twelve points I have suggested. There will be particular disagreement, I imagine, on the fourth point; that is, the one concerning free choice.

Not every Humanist wants to use the phrase naturalistic Humanism. Some prefer the term scientific Humanism, secular Humanism or democratic Humanism. There is also a large group who consider Humanism a religion and who therefore prefer the phrase religious Humanism. For my own part, I prefer to call naturalistic Humanism a philosophy or way of life.

25
The Humanist Outlook
ROY WOOD SELLARS

THE HUMANIST OUTLOOK, as I see it, is an affair of cultural growth; a current which has many tributaries. It involves basic cultural and intellectual reorientation of forces that are interacting in a manner consonant with their methods and emphases. On the one hand, I refer to science and philosophy; on the other, to secular movements in social life. I shall illustrate these forces later.

But let me begin not by giving a formal definition of Humanism but by indicating its emphases. It is, I take it, a movement broadly based on cultural trends. It is not abstract but concrete and expresses a reflection on the human condition as it discloses itself in the light of modern knowledge and in the changing patterns of living throughout the world. Man is becoming aware that he is living on a little planet on which he has evolved step by step, biologically and culturally, and that he must stand on his own feet and solve the various problems which confront him and make his life precarious.

It is this orientation that is relatively novel. Traditional religion emphasized a different perspective. Christianity, for example, had a supernaturalistic framework in a three-tier universe of heaven, earth and hell. It inherited this largely from Judaism and added to it a belief in a God-Man saviour and a greater stress on an afterlife. It became a closely woven web of belief, feeling and church organization. In the culture of the time there was little to counteract and challenge it and the result was an Age of Faith. It is the custom of religious thinkers to move within this circle of faith and its assumptions. The Humanist argues that the traditional Christian outlook has been undercut and rendered obsolete by the growth of knowledge about man and his world. He has the positive task of reorientation and of revealing a fresh idea of man's condition and situation in the universe as we are beginning to envisage it.

A brief introductory essay finds itself squeezed for room to say all it wants to say, but before I go further I want to summarize briefly the development of Judeo-Christian theism. The Greeks had their vivid, anthropomorphic pantheon; the Hebrews concentrated on the Mosaic adoption and special covenant. When they came into the land of the Canaanites with their agricultural Baalim, a contest developed with Yahweh not always winning. From this clash came the greater prophets with their moral teachings and the priests with their reformulations of old myths of creation. It was a development toward what is usually called ethical monotheism. Poor Jews! They were always between the upper and nether millstones of great empires and worked out the idea that Yahweh was punishing them for the sin of backsliding. It was a mythological story, but it dominated their lives. Later they contested the early Christian churches as rivals and were given a bad name in the gospels. I am interested in this social history, which is similar in its way to that of America and her tragedy of slavery and racism.

I think it is historically clear, then, that the Jews worked intensively within a mythological framework. It is fascinating to note the stages of their development within this framework to Messianism, thence to Hassidism and Zionism. I have a pupil, a rabbi turned Humanist, who is convinced that their integration in modern culture involves such a shift of outlook.

Looking back at Christian orthodoxy, I can quite understand the motivations leading to the creeds. Jesus, the God-Man, had to be fitted into the celestial scheme of things. There were, of course, schisms and heresies, some of which weakened the Byzantine Empire. The West was less speculative, with Pelagius as an exception. Personally, I admired the universalism of Origen; but many people seemed to desire everlasting punishment for others.

The trouble is, of course, that when Christianity became established there was no countervailing cultural force. This came only gradually with the rise of science. Sir Isaac Newton is an interesting figure since he was deeply concerned with the Bible and yet tended to Arianism, that is, to what became Unitarianism. Out of Newtonianism arose deism with its absentee deity or *Deus Absconditus*. (This is a recurrent theme. I note that the Lutheran

134

martyr to Hitler, Pastor Bonhoeffer, so much admired in clerical circles, thinks that God has left man to make his own way. One might call this a social science form of Newtonian absenteeism.)

Humanism is naturalistic and rejects the supernaturalistic stance with its postulated Creator-God and cosmic Ruler. It regards that traditional outlook as having its roots in Jewish mythology and the support it received in Near East and Hellenistic notions of a dying and resurrected God. (There is no doubt that Paul was influenced in his transformation of Jewish thought by such traditions.)

Semantic hurdles enter here. It is quite understandable that people dislike such frank terms as atheism. Theism has semantic priority. It is supported by religious feeling and tradition. Atheism and godlessness were, on the other hand, terms of opprobrium, but times are already changing, for we hear of the Death-of-God theology, rather a contradiction in terms. Nontheism is a neutral term and may be preferable to atheism. I like to work up from a naturalistic base and put the burden on the theistic outlook. To prove the existence of God has turned out to be a very difficult problem. St Thomas did it to his satisfaction in the cultural outlook of his time, but his assumptions clash with those of the science and philosophy of today and so theologians usually fall back on revelation and encounter. I shall say something about these later.

I am not one of those who oversimplify; and, while I regard the cosmology and ontology of traditional Christianity as completely outmoded, I respect the ingredient which emphasizes love and communal feeling. But we must not forget that the Buddha also stressed compassion and that Confucius recognized the Golden Rule of reciprocity. In its ecclesiastical setting, Christianity was at times blind to this priority. Throne and Altar were often bound together.

I move now to comments on various historical approaches to the Humanist outlook. As I see it, such a move had various stages before it came to a head. There was, first of all, the widening contrast between reason and faith. One can see this even in St Thomas. It broke out at the time of the Renaissance in Italy, in Pomponazzi and Bruno. Cartesian rationalism had its opponents, as in Pascal's appeal to the heart. The silence of infinite space was falling on man.

135

Then came the great eighteenth century with its critical *philosophies*. Science had affected them, though the scientists hardly spoke out. They were on the make and did not want to attract attention to themselves. How different it is today! I want to call attention to the fact that the Enlightenment had a touch of Humanism and charity in its make-up. Marx, despite his emphasis on struggle, inherited these ingredients. That is why we must later put Marxist Humanism in the catalogue of Humanist movements, all, I think, converging on this new orientation of humanity.

Nineteenth century England had a rather subdued culture, called Victorian. The outspokenness of Hobbes was far from it. At best, it set up what it called agnosticism; that is, the view that one does not know ultimate mysteries. It was a defensive stance. I find some Humanists who still call themselves agnostics, especially those who have not come to grips with recent thought in science and philosophy. I myself hold that we have increasing knowledge about our world, and that there is no need to postulate a realm beyond it.

But to continue, let me mention another move toward modern Humanism. The founder of sociology as a science, Comte, worked out a religion in which humanity—past, present and future—was to be worshipped. He was much influenced by the analogy of the Roman Catholic Church and sought sacraments and calendars of outstanding representatives of humanity. I doubt that such an approach is any longer natural to secularistic Humanism. At present the framework of thought and feeling is more concerned with the texture of human living, with procedures and ideals. I take it that the branch of Humanism which calls itself religious Humanism regards its task as that of making adjustments in liturgy and congregational activity. Corliss Lamont has made relevant suggestions here in respect to the ceremonial recognition of death as at once terminal and significant memorially. The dread and anxiety of the existentialists may well be exaggerated, but a proper attitude is a desideratum for both birth and death.

I am now going to shift to the American scene. As I see it, after the deistic move in the colonies receded with the impact of the reign of terror, America indulged itself in successive revivals with disputes between the old lights and the new. Billy Graham is just the latest manifestation of this technique; I recall Billy Sunday. Such men were not theologians and made no pretence to be, they

136

were gospellers of what the British call the evangelical wing. The contribution of the United States was the separation of Church and State and the rise of denominations. Their differences were marginal and are now still less. Perhaps the chief difference was between modernists or liberals, on the one hand, and the fundamentalists on the other. The liberals moved in the direction of a social gospel, but the general framework of belief was the same, a dominant supernaturalism.

I must now refer to my own position. My philosophical thinking led me to a physical naturalism. I had to fit man into the picture and the development of human culture. The result was an outlook which I called Humanism. It seemed to me the logical direction to take. I had never idealized popular religion but took it to be an expression of the need for some conception of man's situation or, as it is usually called now, the human condition. I took it for granted that much mythology and the will to believe operated in it and I recognized the momentum of the past. Yet I felt the necessity of a frank reorientation which I called 'religion coming of age'.

During the 1930s I was invited by a small group of people, teachers and ministers, to give a talk at the University of Chicago on the situation in religion. The outcome was that I was asked to formulate basic principles along humanistic lines. I called my formulation *A Humanist Manifesto*.[1] I sent it back and received suggestions, some of which I incorporated in the *Manifesto*. It was then published with the signatures of many outstanding persons in the religious field, and is now called an historical document. I have found that many do not know of its origin and that is why I give this account.

Then, much to my surprise, there came the incursion, largely from Germany, of what was called neo-orthodoxy and dialectical theology. Barth, Brenner and the Niebuhrs were active agents in this movement; later came Tillich. I have noted some British figures of a similar persuasion. And so the debate began to rage with the clerics in general taking the side of neo-orthodoxy, as one would expect.

This stance meant a stress on revelation as a source of information about God's intentions. The latest version of this outlook is a cult of a mysterious encounter, cherished in religious circles. While I am not a positivist, I would support their stress on verification.

[1] Sellars, Roy Wood (1933), 'A Humanist Manifesto' in *The New Humanist*, **VI**, 3.

Besides, as I see it, revelations and encounters are tied in with supernatural frames of discourse running counter to hard-earned knowledge about man and his condition. As in Job, the God of revelation never told man anything about the world, but stood on his pride of place. As I see it, neo-orthodoxy is a sort of wishful movement, quite understandable historically. But interestingly enough, neo-orthodoxy lost its momentum and its language began to sound somewhat archaic. What was this God beyond popular theism? And how did Christology fit into the scheme? This is, after all, the age of science and technology. Man is beginning to stand on his own feet and face his social problems. And they are increasingly difficult ones.

Changes are very rapid these days. I remember when secularism was the great enemy of Christianity. In his book *The Secular City*,[2] Harvey Cox of the Harvard Divinity School welcomes it. He celebrates the city's liberties and stimulus. Rural Christianity is giving way to urban life. I wish, however, that Cox had paid more attention to the situation in American philosophy and had not been so conventional in his emphasis on German thought with its existential vaguenesses.

I think we have convergence in Felix Adler's ethical societies, in Freudian psychoanalysis and in Marxism. Adler was a forerunner and pioneer who gave up the rabbinate for secular philosophy. His stress was then on education and reform, on 'deed rather than creed'. I have the impression that the ethical movement converged on Humanism in a sort of inevitable way, a recognition of like-mindedness.

Freud was, in his way, a rationalist warning against such illusions as the projection of the father image into the cosmos. He was critical of an introjected conscience and, like Socrates, stressed self-knowledge with *id*, *ego* and *superego* functioning together. The result of this was a depth psychology recognizing stages in the growth of the individual, and possible lapses. The climate of all this was humanistic in tone, so that here, too, we find convergence in our culture.

I come next to Marxist Humanism. As I have already mentioned, its roots go back to the Enlightenment. Marx and Engels were also influenced by Feuerbach, that deviant from Hegelianism, who saw at the base of religion man's alienation from himself. Man, self-

[2] Cox, Harvey (1965), *The Secular City*, New York: Macmillan.

transcending as no other animal is, generates the belief in an 'Other' and assigns to Him all man's good qualities and to himself much that is evil. This projection demands control or it may work havoc through persecution. Marx argued that Feuerbach neglected social history with its antagonism; did not religion operate only too often as an opiate of the people? In Russia, Lenin noted the intertwining of Church and state. But I see that revisionism in what may be called Socialist Humanism is more openminded; there is a touch here of religious Humanism.

I should, of course, mention the work in Humanism of the famous biologist Sir Julian Huxley, who turned away from agnosticism to stress scientific method and the scientific outlook on the world. I cannot see that the adjectives used make much difference—naturalistic Humanism and scientific Humanism are much the same. I merely mention the additional fact that we are increasingly aware of the ecological dimension of human life, man's interaction with nature for good or ill.

All these movements converge towards a Humanist outlook. Quite understandably, the debate will long continue. Yet it is clear that new directions are at work in man's consciousness the world over. He increasingly recognizes that his destiny is in his own hands.

To return to the semantic clarification of the term Humanism as concerned with humanity's situation and condition, I would simply emphasize the naturalistic setting so common these days to both science and philosophy and, within it, stress the need for man to face up to the demands of his life in politics, economics and morals. Here we have matters of ultimate concern and it is well to grasp them realistically. But this does not exclude the desire for human happiness and self-expression, as in human relations and art. Rather, the social sciences must recognize and include these desires. In my first book on the topic, which I called *The Next Step in Religion*,[3] I had such emphases and reorientation in mind and sought to naturalize the term 'spiritual' in terms of human virtues and values. What is the nature of the human spirit? Is it transcendental, or empirical and quite of the stuff of human living?

The point the Humanist would make is that a new orientation in our culture is under way and has science, technology and, I believe,

[3] Sellars, Roy Wood (1918), *The Next Step in Religion*, New York: Macmillan (out of print).

philosophy supporting it. There is much to be done in the domain of human values, personal and social. The human spirit must concentrate on its table of values and define the spiritual in this context. It is a demanding and worthy task.

26
Contribution to a
Definition of Humanism

MATHILDE NIEL
translated by Henry Darcy

HUMANITY FINDS ITSELF at present in an agonizing situation. The species is threatened by nuclear confrontation, conflict and the destruction of the biological equilibrium of the planet. The breakdown of human values and the dehumanization of an urbanized world have produced in youth a moral and spiritual distress without precedent. In many countries, freedom of the individual and human dignity are despised. Democracy retreats before the offensive of different ideological passions. Egoism and the blindness of the rich countries have driven the poor Third World to despair and revolt. Never has the problem of man's existence, future and happiness been posed with such acuteness. Never has Humanism been as necessary as today. Never have Humanists been obliged to carry on their shoulders such heavy responsibilities.

At this critical moment of history, when the sole hope of humanity resides in putting the aims of Humanism into practice, those who call themselves Humanists have the duty to clarify their ideas in the light of historical experience and science and to devise the most appropriate action. It is, therefore, necessary to redefine Humanism and to unite all efforts to arrive at a total vision which is as complete and as precise as possible.

From the sixteenth century on, the word Humanism has not been limited to the meaning imputed to it by the ancients, even though the Humanist spirit corresponds to the Humanist interests that had their roots in antiquity. Throughout history, the diverse Humanisms (those of Socrates, the Stoics, the Christians, Erasmus, the philosophers of the Enlightenment, Socialism, etc.) have always been based on respect for the human person, on confidence in man, his reason and his possibilities of improvement. In opposition to these positive tendencies, the subjection of man, partisan passions and divisive conflict may be considered to be anti-Humanist.

Humanism and anti-Humanism are not new phenomena. They both had their inception long ago in the history of man and they have always more or less coexisted. Thus, certain passages of the *Book of the Dead* of the ancient Egyptians ('I have provoked no tears'), the messages of Socrates ('Evil is ignorance'), of Buddha ('If hate responds to hate, however shall hate be ended?'), of Jesus ('Thou shalt love thy neighbour as thyself'), among many others, are early Humanist messages. But equally humanistic are technical and scientific inventions and works of art (when they are not put in the service of destructive powers) and all the manifestations of solidarity among men, whether individual or institutional.

Unfortunately for the individual and his self-realization, individual and collective ambition, domination and subjection, distrust and hate, conflict and war came into existence with the development of the first cities. The ancient idolatries of the clan, family, divinity and the city are anti-Humanist, as are modern idolatries of the nation, ideology and technology, which alienate the individual, form barriers between men and engender conflicts of violence.

We have seen in our epoch that anti-Humanist forces take many forms and that they have become particularly dangerous. Some among them are so pernicious that they cover themselves with the mask of Humanism. In the name of an absolutized and deified Man, and in the name of the Humanist ideas of liberty, justice and fraternity, those in power in certain countries despise and sacrifice human values of the present-day man for a future society without conflict. And it is in these names that the present world is maintained in a constant state of cold war or open war under the menace of terrifying weapons.

Some find in technology an omnipotent deity on which they count to liberate the individual in the future. But the same people willingly sacrifice the life of present-day man to the machine, and they accept an ugly and dehumanized environment.

Sharing the same aim to render the man of tomorrow perfectly happy in a perfect society, certain philosophers (for example, Herbert Marcuse), followed by despairing youth, accept intolerance, disdain reason and exalt subjectivism and violence. Others (for example, Michel Foucault) go as far as to predict the death of the

142

subject and of human liberty. In the West, disoriented by the crisis of values, the dehumanization of industrial and capitalist society and the failure of revolutionary ideals, youth has lost faith in man, reason and life and hides the anguish in mystical collectivistic experiences and in the search for an artificial paradise. If one adds to all this the lack of conscience which has allowed the Third World to fall deeper and deeper into poverty, and which has abandoned to totalitarian forces (for their own profit) the legitimate revolt of millions of men, there is good reason to be pessimistic about the realization of the goals of Humanism.

However, at the same time, one sees in the Western countries and in certain countries of the East the beginning of a humanistic rejection of authoritarianism and bureaucracy. One speaks of 'socialism with a human face' (even if the realization of this has been smothered at birth). One speaks of 'self-actualization', 'participation', and 'dialogue'. If these words are often utilized for political purposes, it is nonetheless true that the world as we know it—the world of segregation, totalitarianism and destructive conflicts—is being shaken to its foundation. Youth very often rejects the *status quo*, while a new world—a world of the expression of self and of human solidarity—struggles painfully to see the light of day. In other words, people are beginning to demand that Humanist values, which were Humanist ideals until now, be effectively lived by both the individual and society.

Certainly we are still dealing here with vague aspirations, a feeble light in the present-day gloom. The forces of anti-Humanism are far from having been disarmed, and the demystification related to alienated values engenders more anxiety and disorder than freedom and a humanized order. Nevertheless, this aspiration for a *lived* (rather than an absolute) Humanism can help us define today's Humanism. It can permit us to search for the causes of the present-day retreat of Humanism and to find the conditions that a renovated Humanism must produce in order to make a new beginning.

Any discredit to Humanism today comes perhaps from its excessive idealism. Perhaps it has always had too much confidence in man, in his reason and in his good will. Perhaps it has misunderstood the complexity of the human soul, the power of passion and the depth of alienation. Perhaps it has ignored the attraction which man has for domination and his need to erect in absolute terms his ideas and his sentiments, hating and fighting those who seem opposed to his own values. Too moralistic and insufficiently psychological, Humanism, perhaps, has misunderstood the fact that man cannot discard his absolutist, segregationist tendencies without having experienced a different life in which he is allowed to express his creativity and his solidarity. In our epoch, it no longer suffices to be a Humanist in thought and in the solitude of one's conscience. It is necessary to be a Humanist in practice and with others. It is necessary to prove that the practice of humanistic values renders man more happy than domination and the pursuit of absolutist values. In other words, Humanists are not uniquely confronted by a moral problem or by an economic and social problem, but by a psychosocial and practical problem very difficult to resolve.

Psychology tells us that man cannot achieve the Good by freedom of the will and free choice, as religion and morality teaches. Man spontaneously performs the Good, if he has been awakened since earliest childhood to humanistic ideals and has been educated practically to autonomy and solidarity inside the family and in the school. Man spontaneously performs the Good if he participates freely in the life of the community because it respects, encourages and integrates his autonomy, and if the community itself becomes creative due to the free creativity of its members. Sentiments of liberty, fulfilment and fraternity spring spontaneously from the continuous exchange between the autonomous, creative individual and the open society.

Some have pretended that changes in the economic and social systems in turn produce changes in man. But we discover that once the revolution is accomplished and the economic system transformed at the price of immense suffering, the former alienation reappears in the form of will-to-power and aggressive nationalism; for the revolution was accomplished by alienated men who have remained imperialistic. Others pretend that men can freely do the Good, whatever the social conditions. They forget that bad education, poverty, dehumanized work and various forms of subjection destroy not only creative potentialities but also the capacity for fraternal love, which is transformed by revolt, hate and destruction. It is for this reason that Humanism must aim to change the social system based on segregation and conflict and, at the same time, seek to develop the talents and the autonomy of the individual.

During this period of searching and transition Humanism must base itself on *scientific knowledge* of the psychosociological causes of alienation. Humanists must concentrate on these problems and awaken other men to the objective critique of the value of their society. Films, the press, literature and political discourse must pass the crucible of Humanist criticism. It is necessary to learn to discriminate among the diverse forms of human and anti-human language.

But the rational and scientific critique of language and values would not suffice if it were not accompanied by an emotional impetus, a 'Humanist faith', which allows us to retain confidence in life, man and his destiny, and to continue to think and act. This faith must go beyond deficient religious beliefs and must replace the scepticism or the growing mystique of political inspiration, whether religious or commercial. It must give back to man the forces of creation and friendship that are in him, even though they are often ignored and suppressed. The Humanist faith is a rational faith because it bases itself on the facts and the realities evident to all: for example, the creative power of thought as manifested in civilization in the form of technical, scientific and artistic inventions; the destructive character of absolutism and fanaticism, the capital rôle of man in terrestrial evolution. For the Humanist faith, conscience does not constitute an isolated phenomenon in the universe; it is an integral part of man and life. Conscience, far from being a void which we attempt to fill (J. P. Sartre), constitutes a creative drive to synthesis, which, if not hindered by absolutist aspirations and messianic aspirations, tends to connect the individual to life, to the world and to the infinite.

Thanks to the knowledge of human needs, the scientific critique of values, the affective and rational élan and to a technical progress that can provide the material basis of liberation, it is possible to begin today to construct a planetary civilization. Here human values would no longer be erected as absolutes but would finally be lived by men who would feel themselves free in the practice of life. Of this new Humanism, we propose a definition which can only be imperfect and temporary. In any case, Humanism is not itself a fixed value. Its definition can be only a synthesis that springs from the confrontation of diverse definitions. It is in this way that the definition herein proposed could give place to a first synthesis that would have to be constantly corrected in the light of the progress of knowledge and the experience of life.

Humanism is a way of thinking and acting which aims, on one hand, at the liberation of the individual from the authoritarian, absolutist and segregationist spirit, and which attempts, on the other hand, to transform economic and social systems which encourage his alienation. This liberation begins with the scientific criticism of economic and social systems of modes of thought, and systems of education that in the name of absolute values erect incomprehensible barriers and hatred between individuals and groups. In the place of closed hierarchical and competitive societies, Humanism tends to substitute a nonexploitative, fraternal and planetary society. This is a society in which everyone feels himself equal to others, in which no one attempts to dominate others by prestige, power or money, and in which everyone can find his happiness in the fulfilment of self and in collaboration with others.

Humanism does not divide men into 'good' and 'evil'. Liberated from a spirit of opposition, it is interested in all men on the planet and especially those who are materially and spiritually deprived. It tries to find ways to emancipate men from poverty, ignorance and the spirit of segregation. It attempts, therefore, to replace present-day feudal and nationalistic organizations with a supranational organization—a world organization in which there is respect for the human individual and the group.

Humanism is not in itself an absolute, an ideal to be realized in the future. It is above all a form of *practice*. It is necessary to begin now to transform combative individual and social relationships into co-operative relationships and to bring into being new and effective means of action not contradictory to those ends. By such action, animated by a rational faith in man and in life; by scientific knowledge of alienation and the critique of social values; by the creation of open groups inside and outside nations where Humanism is already practised—thus Humanists hope to arrive progressively at a radical transformation of the individual and of social relationships and to an open world society of individual freedom and achievement.

27
Humanism and Atheism
GORA

RELIGIONISTS, SCIENTISTS, AUTOCRATS, democrats, capitalists and socialists are all human. How are Humanists different from the rest of humans?

Humanists respect human personality. They recognize the freedom and dignity of human beings. Non-Humanists, on the other hand, consider human life subject to something supposed to be superior to it. That something may be God, fate, governmental authority, hoary custom, economic condition, material circumstances, historical necessity, cultural milieu, genetic constitution or natural law. Whatever the agent of domination may be, the individual is placed inferior to it. Humanists reject inferiority, as they assert the freedom of the individual. Humanists feel free, while non-Humanists feel slaves.

Because it was a God (*theos*) to which non-Humanists subjected themselves at first, the attitude of subjection came to be known as 'theism'. But theism, in its fuller sense, is not limited to subjection to faith in the existence of God. It connotes subjection in general, not only to God but to government, to custom, to systems, to circumstances or to anything. By and large, theism adopts the philosophy of determinism. According to the determinant, theism is godly or godless. In godly theism the determinant is spiritual and other-worldly. It postulates a set of beliefs in God, soul, afterlife, rebirth and eternal salvation. In godless theism the determinants are mundane. They are political, economic and social institutions and material circumstances. Nevertheless, godly and godless theisms alike enslave the individual to one or the other agent, fetter his freedom and demean his dignity. Prayers to God and petitions to government illustrate the servility of theists. And non-Humanists are theists, since they submit to systems, institutions and traditions.

Humanists are atheists, because they do not submit to godly or

147

godless agents. In positive terms, Humanists assert the freedom of the individual and uphold his dignity. The sense of freedom develops a pattern of life different from the non-humanistic one in which people have been slaves to God, slaves to government, slaves to circumstances and slaves to systems. The Humanist pattern of life keeps man the master of his systems and institutions. The freedom of the individual is the keynote of the Humanist way of life. The difference between the Humanist and the non-Humanist ways of life is the difference between masters and slaves.

Philosophically, Humanists confirm truths rather than stop short with faith and opinions. Workings of human imagination need the distinction between truths and faiths. Imagination forms opinions of things and events which are beyond the immediate reach of the five physical senses. An idea of tomorrow is an example of an opinion. However much opinions are systematized into theories through the disciplines of causal logic and methodology, they can never gain the validity of facts which are known directly. Yet a large part of human knowledge consists of opinions. In real life, these opinions which conform to facts of experience can be regarded as truths; those are false which contradict facts. Verification is the test of truthfulness and unverified and unverifiable opinions are neither true nor false. They are merely opinions which may be believed in at one's own risk. Free imagination without the obligation of verification flies as fancy into the realm of the fine arts.

Non-Humanists mistake faiths for truths. Their minds are closed in blind belief. Humanists keep an open mind. They deem no opinion as truth without verification. Humanists reject faith in God, soul and afterlife, since science shows them unverifiable. There is no room for agnosticism either. The factual experience of the freedom of the individual gives the lie to the assumption of the existence of anything that denies freedom. Obviously, the almightiness of God, the sovereignty of the state, and determinancy of circumstances are opinions affected by the slave-mind.

The character of centralized institutions may create the illusion of their bigness. Verification falsifies their claim. Government is built up by the citizens through contributions of respect for law and payment of taxes. If a considerable section of the people withdraws co-operation and withholds taxes, any government is bound to collapse. Thus the power is with the people and not with the government. Similarly, society is formed by the common under-

148

standing among individuals who can strengthen or weaken the society by increasing or decreasing the common understanding. Outside the common understanding, every individual has his or her private affairs; so the individual is larger than the society. Likewise, material circumstances are but man's tools. Civilization consists in man's progressive control over his circumstances. Natural laws are only man's interpretations of his experiences. Newton interpreted the falling of the apple in terms of gravitation; Einstein read the principle of relativity in the same event; another may explain it differently. Man is the author of natural laws. He is also the author of class, caste, racial, national and cultural distinctions. They change with the change of his mind. Every revolution erases them. Thus man is the master everywhere.

The Humanist realization of the mastership of man brings about a remarkable change in the existing institutions. Non-Humanists submitted to the institutions and allowed unscrupulous men to exploit them in the name of respect for institutions. Consequently, wide inequalities cropped up among the people. But inequalities are improper and unfair, as all humans belong to the same kind and are similar in structure, strength and talent. Variations in tastes and traits are not only not correlated to claims of superiority of caste, class, race or culture but can be modified and accommodated through training and sympathy. Inequalities between the rich and the poor, blacks and whites, Brahmins and pariahs, dictators and subjects lasted so long because non-Humanists moved blindly along conventional grooves. Humanists see the injustice of inequalities. They can change the outmoded and unjust systems, because they are the masters of systems and institutions. Lack of Humanist consciousness disabled democracy from establishing economic and social equalities in the wake of the political equality contained in the principle of 'one adult, one vote'. Adoption of Humanism is necessary for the success of democracy, and to banish the sectarianism of the political party system.

Humanism improves morality too. Morality is a social necessity; in social relations, the immorality of one disturbs the happiness of another, so free individuals cannot tolerate immorality. Checks and counterchecks ensure morality among free individuals. The rise of freedom and morality abolishes inequalities in three ways. First, those who are in possession of superior advantages realize their moral obligation and share their advantages with fellow-humans.

149

Second, the down-trodden realize their freedom and dignity and refuse to be exploited and enslaved. Third, as the government is common to both the exploiters and the exploited, it is finally compelled to legislate in favour of equality. Intellectual appreciation of a change without practical expression in personal conduct is fruitless. The sense of individual freedom rouses Humanists to accomplish social change by personal effort and example. After all, society is made up of individuals.

Humanists discard violence because it deprives the victims of freedom. The rise of freedom and dignity among the downtrodden disarms violence; what can a tyrant do when soldiers refuse to fight? Humanists resolve conflicts by lifting the dispute to the level of humanness which is common to both the contenders. Class struggles, national wars and racial conflicts are out of place where people feel human.

Humanism is the awakening of the individual to a sense of freedom. Free individuals live equally and morally. But Humanism has not had much impact on social relations, though it has been in vogue for over a century. Wars, class distinctions and race riots have not abated under the influence of Humanism. The reason is clear. Humanists are hesitating to accept atheism, which is the principal feature of Humanism. Without avowed atheism, Humanists compromise with non-Humanist habits and remain academic with little practical use. Atheism activates Humanists, checks immorality and inequality, and keeps vigil on social relations. Vigilant Humanism sweeps away outmoded and unjust systems, institutions, faiths and philosophies, and offers better alternatives. 'Vigilant Humanism' is the need of the hour and atheism supplies the need.

28
Humanism and Marxism

RAYA DUNAYEVSKAYA

MARXISM IS HUMANISM. Despite a hundred-year burial of Marx's Humanist essays, Marx's Humanism has made history, revolutionary history. No other philosophic writing can compare with it. In our era, it was the Hungarian revolution of 1956 that brought Marx's Humanism onto the historic stage. By unfurling the Humanist banner and laying down their lives in the struggle for freedom *from* communism, the Hungarian freedom fighters gave new life to Marx's original definition of his unique world view as a new Humanism or thoroughgoing naturalism, as against 'communism [which] is not itself the goal of human development—the form of human society'.[1] Similarly, the battle of the Czechs for 'socialism with a human face' was Marxist Humanism at its best.

So sweeping was Marx's vision of the new *human* dimension which would unfold in a classless society that he refused, at first, to associate with the then (1844) existing communist sects that he designated 'vulgar' because they thought that all they had to do to achieve a new social order was to abolish private property. Marx's contention was that private property, capitalist private property, had, of course, to be abolished since it was the manifestation of the exploitation of man by man through the instrumentality of the machine. Never again, he continued, must the individual be counterposed to society, for 'the individual is the *social* entity'. Where there is no freedom for the individual, there is no freedom in the society. Unless, however, Marx concluded in those famous 1844 *Economic-Philosophic Manuscripts*, the division between mental and manual labour—that hallmark of all class societies which had become so monstrous under capitalism—were abolished, we would be confronting capitalism under another name!

[1] Bottomore, T. B. (ed) (1963), *Karl Marx: Early Writings*, New York: McGraw Hill, p 167.

What Marx proposed instead was that, in place either of the profit motive of capitalism or the substitution of state for private ownership, the principle of the new society be the freedom of man, the reconstitution of his wholeness, the development of all his innate talents, the unity of mental and manual labour which exploitative society has fragmented, alienating from man not only the products of his labour, but the very activity of labour.

Following is a passage from the chapter 'A New Humanism'[2] which I wrote shortly after the Russian Communist counter-revolution crushed the Hungarian freedom fighters.

> Marx, the Hegelian, had a conception of labour and freedom as *activity*, completely different from the utilitarian conception of the economists, who, *at best*, could see freedom only as satisfied hunger and 'culture'. These—and they include the scientists of our age who see the break-up of the atom, but not the totality of the person—see free time only as 'enjoyment'. Marx saw the free time liberated from capitalist exploitation as time for the free development of the individual's power, of his natural and acquired talents.
>
> He did not consider that Utopia. It was not the hereafter. It was the road to be taken, on the morrow of capitalism's fall, *if* the nationalized means of production were to serve any better end than the privately owned means of production. This too our age can understand more than any previous age, and it is this conception which hangs over the Russian theoreticians like the Sword of Damocles.
>
> Marx must have had them in mind when he criticized classical political economy for wanting to keep the industrial workers' eyes riveted *not* on the vision of total freedom, but on their 'freedom from feudal blemishes'. Marx wrote, 'for them there was history, but history is no more.' For the Russian totalitarians, the Russian Revolution stopped in 1917, and history stopped with the triumph of the One-Party State.

Marx's theory of liberation was unique in still another way which illustrates why this discoverer of what has been called the materialist conception of history insisted on calling his philosophy a new Humanism which, as he put it, is 'distinguished both from idealism and materialism and at the same time constitutes their unifying truth'.[3]

Take the question of religion. No doubt all of you know Marx's famous statement that religion is the opiate of the people. But how many know the context in which the expression appeared? It is one

---

[2] Dunayevskaya, Raya (1958), *Marxism and Freedom: From 1776 Until Today*, New York: Bookman Associates, p64.

[3] Dunayevskaya (1958) op. cit., p206.

of the most beautiful passages in Marx's writings which discloses how *human* was his materialism, how majestic the historic sweep of his demand 'to unmask human self-alienation in its *secular form* now that it has been unmasked in its *sacred form*'. Here is the whole passage.[4]

> *Man makes religion:* religion does not make man. Religion is indeed man's self-consciousness and self-awareness so long as he has not found himself or has lost himself again. But *man* is not an abstract being, squatting outside the world. Man is *the human world*, state, society.... Religion is the sigh of the oppressed creature, the sentiment of a heartless world and the soul of soulless conditions. It is the *opium* of the people. The abolition of religion as the *illusory* happiness of men, is a demand for their real happiness.... Religion is only the illusory sun about which man revolves so long as he does not revolve about himself....

This Humanist view is what compelled him not only to separate himself from the religious view but also from the 'vulgar' atheists. Instead, it was 'the *human world*, state, society' that preoccupied him. Naturally, the human world is primarily concerned with, engaged in, material production. This is what Marx meant by 'material'— the basic and primary conditions of human existence. Rooted in material production, in the relations of men at the point of production, are the legal property relations as well as their philosophic concepts.

'It is not the consciousness of men that determines their existence,' wrote Marx in the most often quoted and most misunderstood statement of his position, 'but, on the contrary, their social existence that determines their consciousness'.[5] There is nothing mechanical about this materialist conception of history; the *truth* that social existence determines consciousness is not a confining wall, but a doorway to the future, as well as an appreciation of the past, of how men moulded history. The Hegelian dialectic, though Marx openly declared it to be the 'source of all dialectic',[6] seemed to limit itself to thought alone as if thoughts were something 'outside' the human being. Marx humanized the Hegelian dialectic. He wrote that same year, regarding the Silesian weavers' strike: 'The wisdom of the German poor stands in inverse ratio to the wisdom of poor Germany.'

[4] Ibid., pp43, 44.
[5] Marx, Karl (1970), *Introduction to the Critique of Political Economy*, New York, Lawrence and Wishart.
[6] Marx, Karl *Capital*, vol. I, p654n.

Pivotal to the Hegelian concept of dialectical development through contradiction and to the Marxian concept of the materialist conception of history is this: the more degraded the worker, the more oppressed, the more alienated, the greater is his 'quest for universality'.[7] In this 'quest for universality', in this striving for freedom and the reconstitution of the wholeness of man, the proletariat transforms reality itself.

Marx's insistence that this was a scientific philosophy was backed up not with factual data alone, but, above all, with historic movement. Thus, in contrast to utopian socialism *and* to mechanical materialism, Marx's view was that there is neither anything 'automatic' about the inevitability of socialism, nor 'glorious' about science; it all depended on the human subject, on the revolutionary compulsions of the proletariat to transform reality by undermining the existing order and creating the new one.

Marx's vision of the pluri-dimensional in man as well as the creativity of his energies and passions—'the energizing principle', he called it—came from the historic concept that *masses in motion*, not individual genius, are both passion for freedom transformed into energy and manifestation of universal 'Reason'. Reason and Revolution are the inseparables in the transformation of reality. Never, for a single instant, did he take his eyes off the actual class struggles that would decide the fate of men. Just as it was men who made religion, not religion men, so it was they who developed science, not science them. The human being, not science, was the stuff of revolution.

Long before Einstein formulated the principle of transformation of mass into energy, stating that all elementary particles are made of the same stuff—energy (as against the nineteenth century concept of matter, the twentieth century holds that 'matter exists because energy assumes the form of elemental particles')[8]—Marx warned against the *direction* science had been taking. A century before the atom was split and released, not so much the greatest energy force on earth as the most destructive, Marx wrote in 1844: 'To have one basis for life and another for science is *a priori* a falsehood.'[9]

---

[7] Marx, Karl (1963), *Poverty of Philosophy*, New York: International Publishers.
[8] Heisenberg, W. (1959), 'From Plato to Max Plank' in *Atlantic Monthly*, November.
[9] Bottomore (1963), op. cit., p164.

We have been living this lie ever since, with the result that man faces his own destruction, not just figuratively, but literally. The destructive forces come not only from science, but from the class structure of society. Indeed, it is the class structure which determines the direction of science, even as it is this class structure which spews out racism in its death throes.

Nowhere is the *today-ness* of Marxist Humanism more sharply delineated and relevant to the problems of our day in America than on this question which will reveal to us as well the American roots of Marxism.

Truth is always concrete, wrote the most idealist of bourgeois philosophers, Hegel. In practising that principle, the most revolutionary philosopher, Marx, appeared 'nonmaterialistic' to the self-styled American Marxists who tried evading the actual Civil War by covering themselves with the abstraction that they were opposed to 'all slavery, wage and chattel'.

Marx's reply to these would-be adherents was that, if this was Marxism, *he* was not a Marxist. Truth is always concrete. The greater affinity of ideas turned out to be between Marx and the American Abolitionists, regarding both their total opposition to slavery and their recognition that what defaced America could be regenerated only through association with black revolutionaries. Or, as the great New England Oppositionist Wendell Phillips put it, Oppositionists were ten feet tall because they stood on the shoulders of the Negro slaves following the North Star to freedom.

Long before civil war was in the offing, Marx argued that intellectuals were held in tow by the ruling class in their unawareness of the origins of language itself and use of certain words. Thus, they used the word 'Negro' and the word 'slave' as if they were synonyms. 'A Negro is a Negro,' Marx argued. 'He only becomes a slave under certain conditions,'[10] conditions created, not by them, but by their exploiters, who, furthermore, exuded the racist language as rationale for the continuation of slavery.

The year was 1847. By the time John Brown led the attack on Harper's Ferry, Marx wrote to Engels on 11 January 1860 that the biggest event in the world was 'the movement of the slaves in America started by the death of John Brown'. When, the following year, civil war finally broke out, Marx threw himself into the battle by spreading the words of the American Abolitionists in England

[10] Marx, Karl (ed), *Selected Works*, vol. I, p263.

and in Germany. The British proletariat had mobilized itself to stop their bourgeoisie from flirting with the Southern oligarchy. Under the impact of civil war in the United States and the strikes in Britain and France, as well as the Polish rebellion, the first International Working Men's Association was established, with Karl Marx in its leadership.

Nor was the International's support of the North limited to writing letters to President Lincoln, or even extolling Abolitionism. No, it transformed, that is to say, made more concrete Marx's concepts of labour's self-development, by extending them to the question of race: 'Labour in the white skin cannot be free so long as labour in the black skin is branded.'[11] This was not mere rhetoric. Marx proved its truth by showing that it was only after the abolition of slavery that the first national trade union was established in the United States. And this National Labour Union, headed by Sylvis, soon joined the International Working Men's Association. Deep indeed are the American roots of Marxism. Their long burial can no more exorcise them from American history than the exorcism of the true history of black revolt could withstand today's tidal wave of revolts.

Marx at first had called his philosophy a new Humanism; then, with the 1848 revolutions, on the eve of which he had written: 'A spectre is haunting Europe—the spectre of Communism', he had changed the name to Communism. That there was no change in Humanist concepts is clear from this same history-shaping *Manifesto* which also declared: 'The free development of each is the condition of the free development of all.' And when 'all' meant not only all men in any one country or even continent, but the world, he changed the name again, this time to the International Working Men's Association. That remained the name after its headquarters moved from London to New York and until his death, for his Humanism meant that the many worlds were one and this one world was moving towards full liberation.

When the new, third world came onto the historic stage in our postwar world, it, too, singled out the Humanism of Marxism as the philosophy that governed it. As Leopold Sedar Senghor expressed it in the international symposium on *Socialist Humanism* that, for the first time, brought together not only the Humanists from East and West, but from the South and North: 'Beyond the economic

[11] Marx, Karl, *Capital*, vol. I, p329.

"appearances", it [Marx's thought] plunges into the *factual* view of things, Marx substitutes a profound insight into human needs. His is a new Humanism, new because it is *incarnate*.'[12]

This exchange of ideas is not new to our age nor even to great men like Marx. It is the innermost hunger of the greatest masses of men. When slave traders were busy establishing the triangular trade of African slaves, West Indian sugar and New England cod, a triangular exchange of *ideas* was established between Africa, the West Indies and the United States (especially with American Negroes). The basic ideas we think of as very recent, such as 'Black is beautiful', were in fact born then. Every idea from black nationalism, 'Negritude', 'African personality' to the 'Humanism of Marxism' was, in fact, born in the nineteenth century.[13] It took us so long to find them only because we do not *listen* to the impulses from below any more than we gather about us the true historic roots of man's struggle for freedom.

You are all aware, I am sure, that Marxist Humanism is not exactly the most popular philosophy in the United States. Whether that or something else is the reason for it not being brought openly into the black freedom movement, there is no way of knowing. But Humanism, in the form of Martin Buber's philosophy, was directly quoted by Martin Luther King in his famous letter from a Birmingham jail, *Why We Cannot Wait*.[14] He referred to Martin Buber's most famous expression of his philosophy, the 'I-thou' relationship, and said that until Americans recognize that the question of segregation is not an 'I-it' relationship, that is to say, not a relationship of a person to a thing, but an 'I-thou', a human relationship, segregation will not be abolished. Where King did not directly mention Marx, the young black revolutionary (such as Eldridge Cleaver in *Soul on Ice*)[15] is openly invoking the name of Karl Marx. The frozen lines of communication between black and white can be reopened only through such a total philosophy of freedom as Marx's Humanism. Without the red colouration, the name for 'the man' is 'whitey' who has so repulsed the black freedom fighter that he has no desire

[12] Senghor, Leopold Sedar, 'Socialism is Humanism' in Fromm, Erich (ed) (1967), *Socialist Humanism*, New York: Doubleday, p61.

[13] Dunayevskaya, Raya (ed) (1963), *American Civilization on Trial*, Detroit, Michigan: News and Letters Committees, 1st ed. May; 2nd ed. August, 1970.

[14] King, Martin Luther (1965), *Why We Cannot Wait*, New York: Harper and Row.

[15] Cleaver, Eldridge (1969), *Soul on Ice*, London: Cape.

for any dialogue with him. In that case, just as surely as the H-bomb has called the very survival of mankind into question, so has the colour division.

On the other hand, because of the all-pervasiveness of the alienations in all strata of the population, stretching across the generation gap as well, the very totality of the crisis impels a search for new beginnings. Hence, there is that shock of recognition as we come face to face with the Humanism of Marx, who, from the start of his break with bourgeois society, held that the overthrow of the old is insufficient for the creation of the new unless we thereby release the vast untapped energies of millions upon millions of the oppressed and degraded and thereby add a new dimension to man himself.

Marx lived in just such a time of crisis as we are witnessing today. That is what makes him so contemporary. He has something to say to us. Let us listen. Marx was asked why he had broken with the bourgeois society into which he had been born; what need he had to become a radical. His answer was that no man is whole when the social order is so alien; and to end alienations one must become a radical, for 'To be a radical means to grasp something at its root. The root of mankind is man.'

It still is.

29
Zen and Humanism
BERNARD PHILLIPS

ZEN IS THREE THINGS. First, externally and objectively considered, it is a particular sect of Buddhism. As such, it has its own history and institutionalized forms. Second, from a deeper point of view, it is the heart and essence of Buddhism, having no doctrine or scriptures of its own but pointing to the ultimate source of all Buddhist teaching, namely, the enlightenment experience of the Buddha. On this level, it is a discipline oriented towards gaining for the disciple, in the context of his own life, that illumination of mind, pacification of the heart and freedom of action that the historical Buddha achieved through his enlightenment. Third, and still more profoundly considered, Zen transcends the particularities of Buddhism as such and is not one religion so much as it is religion itself in its most universal intention. In other words, it is the life of truth, of authentic being, wherein the self has overcome its alienation from itself and from all other things. When Zen in this sense is fully concretized, there is no longer anything to be called Zen, and the uniqueness of Zen is that when it is realized it bows out of being. Life in its unconditioned integrity calls for Zen no more than water calls for wetness or fire for heat.

Humanism has signified many things, but most essentially it is a concern with man and a faith in the adequacy of human resources—intelligently employed—to actualize the promise and splendour of human life.

There is a continuing ambiguity in Humanism stemming from the absence of unanimity among Humanists as to what constitutes the 'human'. All metaphysical thought is finally directed to clarifying the mutual status of nature, man and God; and the Humanist has finally to declare his own understanding of the matter.

In fact, some Humanists have felt more comfortable with God than with nature, while others are more fearful of God than of nature. And thus it is that, historically, Humanism has fought its war now on one front, now on the other, for the middle ground it chooses to occupy has been perennially imperilled by two rival imperialisms. Humanism has striven to preserve the independence of the human *vis-à-vis* the divine; it has also battled to guard the human against the rawness, brutishness and darkness of nature. At the beginning of the modern epoch, the 'humanities' were upheld against the 'divinities'. In more recent times, and by such Humanists as Matthew Arnold, Irving Babbit and Paul Elmer More, the 'humanities' have been championed against the encroachments of the natural sciences.

As a matter of practical strategy, shall man direct himself primarily to *natur*, to *kultur* or to *geist?* What are man's ultimate needs? Are they to be met by enlarging his mastery over nature? Do they demand as well the culturing of restraints and capacities in himself that are uniquely human and not in the ordinary sense natural? Or, and beyond all these, is there in the human heart an irrepressible longing for an overcoming of the alienation from its own ground?

As a pedagogy, Zen is a pointing to the Zen beyond Zen, and that is nameless and uncharacterizable from the outside and abstractly in as much as it is concretion and inwardness. It is living and livable and the source of life.

Zen in this ultimate sense is both like and unlike Humanism. In the same way, a loaf of bread is both like and unlike every photograph taken of it from whatever angle. The bread, unlike the photographs, is meant to be eaten, and it sustains life. Just as the bread is neither a view nor a composite of views, so is Zen beyond Zen not a position or a point of view. No 'ism' has the power to nourish life. Only realities fuel life; viewpoints and philosophical positions can point only as a menu points to a meal.

As 'isms' Zen Buddhism and Humanism are equally abstractions. What redeems Zen even on this level, however, is its clear awareness of itself as an abstraction. It does not seek to perpetuate or to propagate itself as a system. It does not compete with other systems for formal adherents. Its very nature is provisional, and there is only an intermediate and pedagogical meaning to the notion of 'being a Zen Buddhist'. 'Being a Zen Buddhist' has no intrinsic significance nor any sacramental value. It is only a temporary designation for one who is en route towards the goal of discovering his nameless self, and thus of transcending anything that could be labelled 'Zen'.

160

A true man of Zen takes everything as grist for his mill—even the mill—so he will finally want to grind up even his Zen. Or, to change the figure, Zen is only a soap. Soap is needed to loosen the dirt on the skin, but if the soap is allowed to remain, it becomes another kind of dirt. Therefore, you must wash off both the dirt and the soap; then you will be really clean. Otherwise, you will have 'the stink of Zen'. True Zen is then a return to a state of purity in which any residual Zen would only be another impurity. In the Eden of Zen man is in his primal nakedness and all coverings are superfluous, even garments woven of Zen.

What about Humanism? Is it similarly oriented towards its own eventual dissolution? Or is it a position not ever to be renounced but clung to for the sake of an identity? Does Humanism aspire to bring its adherents into a state of purity that is beyond Humanism as it is beyond every other 'ism', and where they are no longer this or that but just themselves, needing no label and seeking no longer to gain an identity through affiliation with an abstraction?

Ultimately, it is a question of the basis of identity. The mystery of man is that his true identity is not merely a natural datum; it has to be created and discovered. If the identity he rests in is only nominal or conventional, then it is simply a rôle assigned or assumed, the alternative to which may be felt as an abyss of nonentity. The identification with a position, a party or a particular self-image is in that case maintained as a shield against the threat of nothingness. The identity gained through occupying a position is in the last analysis only a pose or a posture.

Is there such a thing as *real* identity?

The question put by the Psalmist is, 'What is man that Thou art mindful of him?' But for Zen, the ultimate question is not 'What is man?' but 'Who am I?' Insofar as I encounter myself solely through an answer to the first question, I do not deal with myself as myself but only as an instance of something general. But the question 'Who am I?' asks me to take hold of myself in my particularity and not simply as an instance of X. The answer to the first question can be set forth in words; the answer to the second question—if it is a real answer and not an escape into a generality—emerges only when the self encounters itself.

Who am I? Until this is answered, we live and move and have our being in an anxious darkness. When this is answered, when we possess our own souls in truth, then we can live and die with our knowledge and our ignorance of other things. This is the holy wisdom, Nirvana, the kingdom of heaven, the priceless pearl, and in comparison with it, what currently passes for *philo-sophia* is a form of self-forgetfulness or self-evasion.

Zen is not psychotherapy as that is ordinarily understood. To know about yourself may be useful or necessary but it is not the same thing as knowing yourself. In knowing about yourself there is still some distance between the knower and what he knows. In Zen there is no distance and no objectification of the self to itself. So Zen would rather say 'Be thyself'. To stand outside myself and to inspect myself is to divide myself into knower and known, and no knowledge stemming from a divided self can ever yield wholeness or be a sufficient basis of integrity in word or deed. In a self-knowing involving a duality of knower and known, the self-as-knower still wishes to hold on to and control the self-as-known.

But Zen completely disallows any duality, which means the true self is never found where the self-as-object is held before the self-as-subject. In wholeness there is no holding up a part of the self. Everything must be surrendered, even the act of surrendering. This is where Zen goes beyond any religion that enjoins the self-denial and giving all to God. Zen would also say deny God, deny the deniers of God, deny thyself, deny thy other and deny all denying as well as all affirming. What then remains when both God and the Devil have been left behind; when we are neither Buddhists nor non-Buddhists, Humanists nor non-Humanists; when we have killed the Buddha and all the patriarchs and can live either in heaven or in hell? In short, what is left when everything nameable has been left behind?

In reply to all his disciples' probings for light on ultimates, we have the Buddha's gentle smile.

When Pilate asked, 'What is truth?' Jesus was silent.

To the query, 'What is Brahman?' the Upanishads answer, 'Not this, not that.'

To Moses' request after His name and definition, Jehovah responds, 'I am that I am.'

And when Bodhidarma stood before the bewildered Chinese emperor, and the latter asked, 'Who is it that stands before me?' Bodhidarma said only, 'I know not, sire.'

All pure Zen, as is likewise the first statement of the *Tao Teh Ching*:

The Tao that can be spelled out is not the eternal Tao.
The name that can be named is not the real name.

Humanism is a stand. Zen is neither the affirmation of a stand
nor the denial of any stand. Humanism is a position *vis-à-vis* alternative positions; it affirms some things to be true and denies others.
Zen is not to be found in the realm of assertion and denial, of
proof and disproof, of belief and disbelief. It is not anything one
can be either for or against. Whether one is for it or against it,
one is *ipso facto* outside it and not in touch with it. As the Sixth
Chinese Patriarch put it: 'There is nothing to argue about here.
Any argument is sure to go against the intent of it.'

The philosopher whose relation to life is essentially abstract
can think only in terms of positions. But Zen eludes all positions and
all fixing. Positions are only partisan allegiances. If you take sides
you get only a side. The truth of life that Zen seeks is not a side;
it is not a position countered by an opposition. The Zen that is
beyond Zen is not one of several possible alternatives. The alternatives to Humanism are at least conceivable. Zen does not exist
in the realm of opposites or alternatives. Zen is only Zen where
there is no choice, since the chooser and what is chosen are one.
Only Zen can say: 'When me they fly, I am the wings.'

While in its essence Zen is beyond Humanism or any other
'ism', Buddhism has always had a strong component of Humanism
in the sense that it assigns central importance to man and bids
man to save himself by his own efforts. According to Buddhism, it
is only from the human level that enlightenment can be attained,
so that birth as a human being is considered the supreme
opportunity not to be wasted. The Buddha's deathbed charge to
his disciples enjoined them to be lamps unto themselves, to work
out their own salvation with diligence, and not to look beyond
themselves for succour. Although Buddhism subsequently developed
its own luxuriant mythology, as it came from the Buddha it had
no concern with objectified superhuman entities. But even where
there is subsequent reference to such, they rank below the enlightened man; and the Buddha is titled 'Teacher of gods and men'.

In Zen it is stated that before enlightenment, the Buddha was an
ordinary man. After enlightenment every ordinary man becomes
a Buddha; and again, that if there were no men there would be no
Buddhas. All in the spirit of Humanism.

163

On the other hand Buddhism in general and Zen in particular cannot be equated with Humanism. Zen is religion, which is to say it possesses what Humanism lacks, namely cosmic rootage. Enlightenment is not solely a psychological or moral transformation. It is not simply the replacing of one finite state of being by another. It is an overcoming of the dualism of finite and infinite, of the alienation of the finite from its ground, which is to say it has a spiritual dimension as well as a humanistic or moral one.

For Humanism the proper study of mankind is man. But men vary; and from where are we to derive the norms defining what is truly human? Is 'true manhood' (to use one of the translations of the term *Jen,* which is the foundation stone of Confucian Humanism) to be encompassed in any definition, or is it something that needs only to be lived in order to be known? Or in other words, as far as goodness is concerned, does essence precede existence or vice versa? Why is it that such existential Humanists as Confucius and Socrates are not prepared to answer their pupils' inquiries with an abstract definition of manhood or virtue?

Aristotle, in his *Ethics,* states that the good is what the good man does. This means that the good man is the criterion of the good, rather than vice versa, and that the good is only an abstraction from the living man of goodness. If that is so, what is crucial is not so much the theoretical inquiry: 'What is the good?' but rather the existential inquiry addressed to oneself: 'How do I become a good man?' What might have been the subsequent course of Western thought if Aristotle had taken a parallel stand in his *Metaphysics* and had similarly stated that the real is what the real man is? This would have meant that Being is not to be grasped speculatively but is only to be entered into existentially. One knows reality to the extent that one is real, and the problem is not to formulate an objective and formal criterion of reality, but to be real oneself. That is, the question for a Zen Aristotelian is not: 'What is Being *qua* Being?' but 'How do I contact my own true Being?'

Zen's approach to true manhood may be gathered from the following story.

> Rinzai once stood before his monks and said, 'There is one true man with no title who presides over this reddish fleshly mass of yours. He is all the time coming in and out through your sense organs. If you have not yet testified to the fact, look, look!'

A monk came out of the ranks and asked, 'Who is this true man with no title?'

Rinzai then came down from his straw chair and taking hold of the monk he said, 'Speak, speak!'

The monk was paralyzed and speechless, whereupon Rinzai let him go, remarking, 'What worthless stuff is this true man of no title.'

Everything in Zen is directed to awakening the person to the realization of his true identity with the 'true man with no title'. 'No title' means, of course, not to be pigeonholed or conceptualized, not limited by any form, hence not either to be defined or confined.

The 'man of no title' has no residue of anything to be called Zen. He is unclassifiable and, like the wind, he bloweth where he listeth, and thou canst not tell whence he cometh or whither he goeth. Yet he is not erratic or antinomian. Through being true to his self, the 'man with no title' can not then be false to any man.

The paradox is that where identity can be identified, it is not true identity but only nominal or conventional identity. The man of real identity cannot be identified. He is real, not a label. He does not *possess* an identity, which would then only be a cloak under which he still remains naked. He *is* his identity.

Whether in mathematics or in science, universality is the mark of truth. The truth is that which is true for all, and one who deviates from the truth is not exalted for his individuality. Deviation, if it is not a mark of error, can be only the pioneering of a truth that is intended to be the truth for all.

In poetry, music or painting, conformity is untruth. Self-expression and originality are marks of truth. If all the answers presented to an assigned problem in mathematics are different, not more than one can be right. But in a class in creative writing, if all produce exactly the same composition, not more than one can be a truthful expression. There appear, then, to be two kinds of truth—to one of which individuality is irrelevant and to the other of which it is absolutely essential.

What is the pattern of philosophic truth—is it universalistic and common, or does it incorporate individuality?

What is the pattern of religious truth? Does it allow me to have my own being and truth, or must I wholly conform to a truth beyond myself?

What is truth of being? Is it correspondence with an idea, or is

165

it a truthful relationship with oneself; and if the latter, which self and how does one come to it?

Zen seeks not any kind of propositional truth. It is and has no doctrine, position, code or creed. The man of Zen does not possess a truth. He is his truth.

One of Oscar Wilde's aphorisms asserts that the truth ceases to be true when more than one person believes in it. For Zen, the truth ceases to be true even when one person believes in it.

IX HUMANIST IMAGINATION

30
Ethics and
Humanist Imagination

IF EXISTENTIALISM YIELDS a timeless mood and mysticism yields a
timeless psychology, then Humanism yields a timeless imagination, a universal sensibility.

This sensibility has been variously formulated; a Humanist
imagination works differently in each person who incarnates it.
Thus the sensibility of Humanism is variously expressed—in the
picture of man presented by the Roman poet Lucretius; in the
Stoic philosophy of Marcus Aurelius; in the enlightened paganism
of the fourth-century Roman Emperor Julian; in the Christian
liberalism of Erasmus; in the religion of Confucius; in the novels
of George Eliot; in the liberal Unitarian theology of Theodore
Parker; in the neo-Kantianism of Felix Adler; in the sculpture of
Rodin; in the music of Frederick Delius; in the essays and novels of
Albert Camus; in Pope John's *Pacem in Terris*.

One important dimension of Humanist imagination is the dimension of novelty and hope. On her election to the Belgian Academy
in 1936, the French writer Colette said to the assembled literary
gentlemen: 'I became a writer without noticing the fact and
without any one else's suspecting it. . . . You must not pity me
because my sixtieth year finds me still astonished. To be astonished
is one of the surest ways of not growing old too quickly.'

The ability to see familiar things freshly, not to be deterred by a
memory of unfortunate events in the past—this is a great gift and
Colette was among the few who had it in abundance. Her capacity
to be astonished, to notice the daylight beginning to touch the
arches of the Palais Royal as though she had never noticed it
before, remained so strong for the eighty-one years of her life that
it became a kind of magic. The ability to be astonished confers
purpose, the motivation and power to work for change. The

phenomenon of hope is made possible by the capacity and courage to take one's future in hand. If change is precluded, hope cannot exist.

Only man can hope because he is not bound by instinctual behaviour alone. And he can hope because he is aware of time and the creative ways by which one can mould the novel possibilities that time carries. As the playwright Ibsen once put it: 'I hold that man is in the right who is most closely in league with the future.'

These considerations lead me into a second dimension, which I shall call the realm of self-transcendence and of excellence. Because man is man, he can, if he wills, stand outside himself, judge himself, get out of the rut of his own ego. Much of daily existence is a running battle between the demands of our egocentricity and the demands of the not-self, of the world external to our ego. Eighteenth century *laissez-faire* philosophy *à la* Adam Smith taught that altruism is the natural result of the free-wheeling egoistic process. That is, if everybody is left alone to pursue his own selfish interests exclusively, society will take care of itself. This is the position of classic liberalism. As the nineteenth century wore on, it became clear that this philosophy was anti-human, anti-humanistic. It was recognized anew that men, because they are men, have moral-social claims upon one another.

I would link the concept of individual maturity to the concept of social responsibility. The person who is tempted to save humanity, but shrinks from direct encounter with individuals is afraid to grow. It is easy to love humanity since that abstraction cannot love you in return. The measure of a man lies partly in the magnitude and character of his temptations. Growing up implies a continual loss of innocence and an increasing awareness of the realities of oneself and of others. As one grows, one shapes a certain distinctive style which enables one to exercise a discriminating openness to experience. And so temptation becomes the portion of one who would grow. No longer to be tempted is to be drained of the ability to transcend, to go beyond oneself.

A man pursues excellence because he can reach ahead of himself, because he respects others and the highest potential of which they are capable. Only a free man can develop true style. The free man is most fully human since he is characteristically absorbed with what he must do and be. The free man's ego, then, liberates him by serving not as an anchor but as a springboard for great living. By travelling in his own style, he makes his life's journey his own.

A third possible dimension of Humanist imagination has to do with scepticism and commitment. Many a self-styled liberal gets into a self-righteous bind when he considers all positions, none of which are wholly satisfactory, and allows himself to be personally committed to none. If he is a member of certain organizations he may try to impose his attitude on the whole group, arguing that the data are insufficient, that we do not know enough to take a stand or some sort of action. Scepticism tends to nourish a passive, indifferent suspension of judgement as it urges us to keep quiet about all matters that are arguable. The very nerve of Humanist imagination, as I conceive it, is courage. Without that, one develops no distinctive style which drives one to participate in history. The ultimate implication of radical scepticism is moral paralysis and social ineffectiveness.

There is nothing inconsistent in being sceptical and being committed. One of the ironies of the human predicament is that virtually any idea man concocts becomes absurd if logically carried to every possible extreme implication. The clever ploy of the radical sceptic is precisely the use of logical reductionism: he points to the least likely and most bizarre, yet logically defensible, implication of an arguable position. But logic and life are not coterminous. Life is always larger than logic.

In short, where action is called for, we must act on what we know. Man is imperfect and fallible by definition, so the absurdity consists in deifying man's given predicament. Man always makes choices and preferences; were he perfect, he would have no agonizing problems in this regard. Only a god has no problems, and man gets into no greater difficulty than when he tries to act—or to not act—as if he were a god rather than a human being.

One in whom a Humanist imagination is embedded passionately believes in the intrinsic worth of man and in his ability to shape meanings by which to live. The Humanist begins and ends with man and is concerned with the life of man penetrating other human lives.

To posit man's intrinsic worth is not to separate it from the worth of all individuals. In short, ethics is implicit. When implications of a humanistic orientation are worked out in the

171

process of living, it becomes an ethical Humanism. Man's search for the sacred—usually equated with the nonempirical—has really been a search for significance. And significance is conceived more and more nowadays in humanistic terms as the quality of human relations whose mainspring is honesty of feeling.

What seems increasingly important is the continual unfolding of man's selfhood in community, the continuous striving to become human. In his novel *Bread and Wine*,[1] Ignazio Silone sees the problem of being human in terms of man's reluctance to face up to the fact of his manhood. The old priest Don Benedetto, speaking to his favourite pupil, Pietro Spina, says: 'No word and no gesture can be more persuasive than the life, and, if necessary, the death of a man who strives to be fair, loyal, just . . . a man who shows what a man can be.'

A Humanist imagination devoid of ethical concern and commitment is self-contradictory. Such an imagination can always inform us about what a man can do and be.

[1] Silone, Ignazio (1964), *Bread and Wine*, translated by Fergusson, London: Gollancz.

Epilogue:
Is Everyone a Humanist?

PAUL KURTZ

THE DRAMA OF AN IDEAL is fascinating. When a daring idea is first proclaimed it is often held to be radical and more often than not it is bitterly ridiculed and attacked. Its critics may eventually concede that the ideal makes a point, though they usually deplore the 'excessive zeal' and 'unreasonableness' of those who advance it. Defenders of the ideal attempt to refine and modify it in order to meet objections and gain converts. Suddenly the ideal may become fashionable, in time everyone may accept it. When the ideal is finally adopted by an establishment, it becomes part of received opinion. It may itself be used to combat new ideals that emerge and threaten. These new ideals are often correctives of the original ideal which, once institutionalized, may have been compromised, even betrayed. Such is the fate of all too many human ideals. They are condemned to suffer the shifting winds of opinion, the tyranny of fads, the hypocrisy of institutionalization. Although they originate as innovative and experimental, they may, unless care is taken, weaken and atrophy with age.

The progress of Humanism typifies the course of moral visions. Originally Humanism was a revolutionary weapon in the hands of free thinkers who demanded freedom from authoritarian ecclesiastical control. Subsequently, Humanism was refined and expanded to express a this-worldly concern for human happiness and for a just and humane society. Today its bitter critics are apparently reconciled to it, for they express agreement with its moral excellences. Humanism has reached its nadir in that almost everyone pays lip service to its ideals and few will dare admit that they do not have a humanistic concern. A graphic illustration of this was the message from Pope Paul VI wherein he proclaims that Roman Catholicism is a 'Christian Humanism' and that the only authentic Humanism must be Christian: 'People today talk of Humanism . . . without Christ there is no true Humanism. . . . True Humanism must be Christian.[1]

And the Second Vatican Council sets forth a Humanism in which 'man is defined first of all by his responsibility toward his brothers and toward history'. Father Vincenzo Miano SDB, of the Vatican Secretariat for Non-Believers, maintains that:

> Every form of Humanism, by definition, wants man to develop all his possibilities and to build a truly human world. Christian Humanism . . . can and must collaborate with *all* men for the promotion of genuine human values . . . Christianity is a Humanism . . . based on God.[2]

The claim that Christianity, and in particular Roman Catholicism, is a Humanism is ironic; for free thinkers, atheists, agnostics, and sceptics adopted the name 'Humanism' in opposition to a dogmatic Church. It is a surprise, therefore, for atheistic Humanists to discover that those whom they had most opposed now proclaim the very ideals that the Humanists asserted in opposition! The irony is compounded when we see that even within the Roman Catholic Church, the so-called liberals who wish to reform and democratize the Church bureaucracy and reinterpret its sterile dogma, do so in the name of Humanism, and that the Pope and Vatican Curia, who often resist such reforms, also insist that Christianity is a Humanism!

The dialectical clash and the fusion of moral ideals can be seen in other contexts: Marx maintained in his *Economic and Philosophic Manuscripts* that he was a Humanist and he attacked modern industrial capitalism for dehumanizing and alienating man. For him the communist revolution was basically a Humanist revolution. Yet his disciples Lenin and Stalin created and institutionalized a new orthodoxy in which Humanism was often betrayed. In Eastern European socialist countries in the past decade, intellectuals and students who have opposed Stalinism have done so in the name of a democratic and Marxist Humanism and of freedom of the individual. Yet at the same time, P. N. Fedoseyev, head of the ideological Institute of Philosophy in the Soviet Union, maintains

---

[1] From Pope Paul's Christmas Message, 25 December 1969.

[2] Miano, Vincenzo, 'A Catholic/Humanist Dialogue' in *The Humanist*, May/June 1971, p. 33.

that communism, i.e. the Marxism-Leninism brand, is the only real Humanism. Fedoseyev says:

> Communists are undoubtedly the most consistent Humanists. Communism is real Humanism. The philosophy of Communism does not tolerate any forms of anti-Humanism, it shall never conclude any ideological truce with them.[3]

And F. V. Konstantinov, another Soviet philosopher, in the same work declares:

> Humanism is a characteristic feature of the consciousness of Soviet man. A man is a friend, brother and comrade to man. This is a principle of Humanism that has asserted itself in Soviet society and in the life and minds of our people. This fact is closely related to the Soviet people's love for peace, their hatred for war-mongers and champions of the arms race. . . . Soviet man is bitterly opposed to conservatism, dogmatism, stagnation; he is imbued with the revolutionary spirit. . . .[4]

Both those who defend orthodoxy and those who oppose it profess the same Humanist ideals!

In Western countries liberal democrats claim to be Humanists, but so do their radical critics—the SDS Port Huron statement of ideals was basically a Humanist document. There are humanistic Protestants and Jews, humanistic Zen Buddhists; indeed, everyone deplores the dehumanizing consequences of modern industrial technology on the quality of human life. Even the most committed Madison Avenue technocratic hucksters emit humanistic slogans as they develop a new concern about ecology and pollution.

Words have a power to capture human imagination. We become the prisoners of rhetoric. Because 'Socialism' has humanitarian and progressive connotations, many people insist that they are socialist—Lenin, Stalin, Brezhnev, Willy Brandt, Jules Moch, Harold Wilson, Mao, Ho and Castro all profess socialist ideals while many of them accuse the others of having betrayed socialism. Even Hitler said that he was a 'national socialist', so as to co-opt a noble-sounding word. 'Democracy' is another example. The United States, China, the Soviet Union, Britain and France all claim to be democratic, but what do they mean by

---

[3] Fedoseyev, P. N. (1963), 'Humanism and the Modern World' in *Philosophy, Science and Man*, Moscow: The Soviet Delegation Reports for the XIII World Congress of Philosophy, The Academy of Sciences of the USSR, p. 27.
[4] Konstantinov, F. V., 'The Individual and Society', *ibid.*, p. 67.

'democracy'? Words which mean all things to all men end up by meaning nothing.

The term 'Humanism' is now an 'in' word. But Humanism is so charged with levels of emotion and rhetoric that its meaning is often vague and ambiguous. It is in danger of being inundated and destroyed by those who do not really believe in it.

Actually the term itself has no 'fixed' meaning. It does not have a Platonic essence in some subsistent realm for which we merely need intuition to understand. 'Humanism' is not a descriptive word but a prescriptive word; that is, it expresses a normative ideal which is offered to guide and direct our conduct. It is not a description of what is the case but what ought to be the case; how we ought to treat human beings, or interpret social institutions and what general model we ought to use for the future.

In a sense, Humanism can mean whatever we want it to. Yet the definition has a descriptive element in that it should enable us to classify those who may properly be called Humanists in the past and in the present, and distinguish them from those who may not. But at root, any definition of Humanism is an ideal definition, for it involves a proposal or recommendation of a normative goal.

We must recognize that Humanism exists in the language stock and that there is a rough body of rules guiding its proper usage. Any new definition that is proposed cannot begin entirely free of existing language patterns. We start with a term already commonly used, but we are not restricted by common usage, especially where common usage is unclear and vague, as is the case with 'Humanism'. Thus we may propose a set of distinctions and rules to clarify and refine the meaning of a term. We may even extend its meaning and stretch it. Terms and words are continually developing and changing, or being modified in the light of new connotations and uses. Since the term 'Humanism' has been used so uncritically, we may redefine it by extending its meaning, and analyzing what is, or ought to be, implicit in it. To refuse to redefine terms because we fear to commit the naturalistic fallacy is already to acquiesce normatively to existing usage. And we can be critical of the normative criteria assumed in ordinary language and extend the range of a word so as to include other criteria.

There is always danger in redefinition—particularly in regard to complex normative terms such as justice, democracy, equality, liberty, where new meanings are constantly being proposed. The

176

danger is that we may become bogged down in 'definitioneering'; that is, we may become advocates of special definitions that are arbitrarily stipulated. If we do so, others may oppose our definition and introduce their own. The open-question argument may emerge: 'Why should I accept your definition and not mine?' The field is thus opened to persuasive definitions and definition-mongering.

Any proposed definition that we wish to introduce must be based, at least initially, upon common usage; but we can go beyond this, providing we give a rational justification for any shifts in application. On the other hand, shifts in meaning which completely undermine the signification of a term are highly questionable. A note of caution: we especially have to avoid the fallacy of emotive mislabelling. We know the emotive effort that can be expended on the easy labelling of people as liberal, conservative, progressive. All such normative terms involve proposals about how we should appraise persons or actions in the future; they are not, we reiterate, simple descriptions of real entities in themselves. The battles for men's moral allegiances often are won by affixing a label. It would be a cardinal mistake to allow the meaning of Humanism to be polluted by its detractors.

Thus we may ask, who is a Humanist and who is not? Surely the term should not be used so widely that it includes everyone, including the anti-Humanist, and excludes no one. Perhaps we ought to begin by negative definition, i.e. by saying what Humanism ought *not* to be considered.

Humanism cannot in any fair sense of the word apply to one who still believes in God as the source and creator of the universe. Christian Humanism would be possible only for those who are willing to admit that they are atheistic Humanists. It surely does not apply to God-intoxicated believers. (This would not exclude a 'religious' Humanism, provided it is a naturalistic non-theism.)

Humanism cannot and should not be identified with a specific political programme, policy or platform. It is not and should not be identified with a particular ideology. It cannot, for example, be identified with the party of progress or revolution as distinct from the party of stability or of order. To define Humanism thus is to restrict its usage too narrowly. If we were simply to identify Humanism with left-wing liberalism or democratic socialism, as some today would have us do, then neither Aristotle nor Hume

177

nor George Santayana could be considered Humanists, for they were decidedly conservative.

Nor should Humanism be equated with an emotional commitment to a vague humanitarianism or the sincere expression of a humane attitude toward other human beings. It is not equivalent to the sentiment of sympathy or benevolence. I have heard Humanists describe an act, deed or person as humanistic or negatively assert that 'a Humanist should surely not behave in this or that un-Humanistic way'. Here there is an identification of Humanism primarily with a purity or honesty of motive and intention. If we were to define Humanism in this way, then Albert Schweitzer, Martin Luther King Jr, St Francis, Pope John, even Jesus Christ, might be considered to be Humanists, even though they were believers. Humanism is not a secularized Christian altruism; and Humanism is not simply 'do-gooderism' at large.

In denying that Humanism and liberalism are the same thing, I am not defending conservatism; and in saying that Humanism and humanitarianism are not necessarily the same thing, I do not deny that one should be generous, altruistic or other-regarding. But the point is that Humanism as a moral concept loses all meaning if no distinctions are made and if its net is cast so widely that it encompasses virtually everyone.

What then should we consider Humanism to be? Under my normative definition I would begin with the following characteristics.

Humanism as a philosophy is opposed to all forms of mythological illusions (religious or ideological) about man and his place in the universe. This means that Humanism involves some scientific view of nature and of man. Any theistic interpretation of the universe and any eschatological drama about divine beginnings and ends is rejected because it is logically meaningless and empirically unverified.

Although Humanism presents a critique of transcendental supernaturalistic theories of the universe, it is not necessarily committed to a specific metaphysical doctrine, except in the broadest sense. It could incorporate, for example, scientific materialism, evolutionary naturalism, organicism or some other metaphysical account based upon science. The point is that it is opposed to metaphysical theories grounded solely on faith or mystery, but it is open to alternative metaphysical explanations.

What is fundamental for Humanism, I submit, is that it be interpreted as a *moral* point of view, one expressing a generalized attitude toward nature and life. If man is a product of evolution, one species among others, in a universe without purpose, then man's option is to live for himself and to discover new areas of significance and achievement. If it is anything, Humanism is an effort at infusing life with meaning and hope. And the Humanist says that if man is aware of what he is and what he is not and is devoid of illusion about his ultimate destiny, then his chief option is to create an authentic life in which some measure of enjoyment and happiness is possible. Man's natural power and resources make him capable of ameliorating his condition and perfecting his life.

This means that he will emphasize self-preservation, creative self-realization and happiness as his chief goals. It means that he will judge institutions and values, organizations and societies by whether or not they deaden, denigrate, destroy or undermine life. He will be opposed to all anti-human and dehumanizing forces that threaten to intrude upon the quality of his experience. He will emphasize all that contributes to his creative self-realization.

Intrinsic to Humanist morality is the desire to allow individuals as free agents to create and guide their own destinies as they see fit. Humanism is related to a doctrine of liberation and emancipation. It values the autonomy of free agents, not only in their intellectual beliefs but in their aesthetic experience, their romantic or sexual proclivities, their moral tastes and values. All men, as free persons, should be accorded some measure of respect, some dignity and value as individuals.

Of course, the Humanist recognizes that man is basically a social agent, and that liberty means nothing unless there is a degree of equality. The demand for equal rights, then, has a claim upon conscience. The Humanist is also committed to democracy, particularly in the present epoch, as an ideal and a method for maximizing happiness and achieving the good society.

However, the Humanist is truly global in his concern for he realizes that no man is a separate island and that we are all part of the mainland of humanity. Thus the idea of mankind as a whole and of one world, is a profound moral vision that sustains and nourishes the Humanist morality. And this can be achieved only by some degree of rule of law, some measure of peace and economic well-being and cultural enrichment for all men, who may share experience and a sense of brotherhood with others. This means that each man is responsible in some sense for what happens to all men, and for the greater community of men. Although we should allow the widest latitude of freedom to individuals to do what they like, we nevertheless recognize the need for the human race to transform blind social forces into rational control and to build a world community.

Thus the Humanist is committed to certain moral ideals. I have provided only a partial list of what they are. Although these moral ideals provide some focus and direction, they are at best general, not specific in character. Humanism becomes mere empty rhetoric and glib generalizations, one might dissent, until it can particularize its principles in practice. However, insofar as it does, it is difficult to say what is the true or authentic 'Humanist' position. For example, should one say that the Humanist is a socialist or a believer in free enterprise, that he believes in student power or faculty control, in high or low tariffs, in welfare programmes or self-help, in the space programme or urban renewal, in the Israeli or Arab cause, etc? Humanists may honestly disagree about each of these complex issues. Thus it is difficult to say exactly what is and is not humanistic. To so limit Humanism would be to destroy it, to make it into a political party or pressure group; yet to refuse to apply Humanism to the great social questions of our time is to run the risk of making it irrelevant. I have no objection, indeed, I would encourage Humanists to be social activists in common with Humanist and non-Humanist friends.

The point is that no one group has a monopoly of wisdom or virtue, nor do Humanists have all the answers to all questions and it would be presumptuous to claim that they did. Humanists do have some important basic points to make and they hope that their fellow men may listen; but humility is a Christian virtue that we ought not to forget, and we have much to learn from others. Some Humanists apparently consider Republicans (in America) and Conservatives (in Britain) to be anti-Humanist almost by definition, but these Humanists are surely narrow and unduly parochial in their outlook, the victims of the political fashions or shibboleths of their age. Humanists should guard against a moralistic sentimentalism that labels a particular plan or policy as humanistic or un-humanistic. Experience teaches that the moral life is at best difficult and that often we have only to choose between the lesser of many evils or to adopt expedient means to achieve good ends. The most surprising lesson to those who assume power is to find that many problems do not lend themselves to the easy solutions that they believed feasible when they were out of power. That is why many supporters of a party or programme often bemoan the fact that their idealistic leaders 'sold out' or 'betrayed them' once they gained power. No, perhaps their leaders have learned only that with the responsibilities of power comes an awareness of the complexities of decision-making.

Like other men, Humanists should be willing to abandon or modify programmes as new facts and social conditions warrant. Yet there are a number of liberal Humanist clichés or myths to which we have succumbed, just as conservatives are often victims of their own mythological dogmas.

Most Humanists have, for example, encouraged the growth of science and technology as the key to the improvement of mankind. Yet who would have thought that the consequences of an advanced technology would threaten to dehumanize and depersonalize man and destroy his natural ecology, so that the moral control of technology has become a vital social concern?

Most Humanists have heralded democracy, believing it to be the hope of mankind. Yet in certain institutions, such as the university or high school, the uncritical application of participatory democracy can lead to the vulgarization of learning and the destruction of standards of excellence.

For decades Humanists have defended sexual liberation and the development of a tolerant attitude towards sexuality. Yet an uncritical interpretation of the new sexual revolution can lead to a bestialization and dehumanizing of sex, the economic exploitation of humans as sexual objects rather than as subjects, and extreme expressions of pornographic pandering.

Humanists have generally been sympathetic to socialism as the wave of the future and many have believed that in changing the conditions of ownership and the relationship of production many or most of the inequities of life can be ameliorated. Yet we have seen that even in socialist societies the oppression of the human spirit and the denial of basic human rights such as freedom of speech and artistic creation can continue, and that with socialism, authoritarian and totalitarian control does not necessarily cease.

Many Humanists have believed that every injustice has a cultural

181

explanation and a social solution. But some inequities may have a biological and genetic explanation, though many Humanists, trapped by a sentimentalist doctrine, refuse to examine the evidence.

Many Humanists worship the myth of Progress, and judge all programmes by whether they contribute to a progressive view of history. Humanists surely ought to work for progressive improvement without personally believing that progress exists in the womb of nature or that there is an inevitable march of human history.

The moral lesson of all this is that we ought to be prepared to learn from experience, not to cling to symbols or slogans (religious or ideological) of the past. We ought to be ready to change, to adapt and to modify our point of view in the light of altered conditions and needs. But we face the same dilemma. Humanism, if it is too general, is empty sermon; if too concrete, it runs the risk of degenerating into a sect or cult or political ideology.

A way out of the dilemma is possible, I submit, only if we add to the above listing of ideals another one which is really, in my judgment, the essential defining characteristic of Humanism or of any point of view that claims to be Humanistic—and what I have in mind here is the centrality of *the ideal of free thought*. For Humanism has always been opposed to any and all forms of tyranny over the mind of man. This puts Humanism squarely in opposition to all authoritarian, religious or totalitarian ideologies that attempt to suppress, limit or censor human intelligence or to impose an orthodoxy of belief or morality. It is opposed to any code of infallibility, official doctrine, Church or party line that is offered as a substitute for free, independent and critical thought and does not permit heresy, dissent or deviation.

Therefore Humanism, if it is anything, is committed to a method of free inquiry and to the use of critical intelligence. If this is the case, then one cannot define the specific Humanist position antecedent to investigation. Indeed, even then Humanists may be expected to disagree vigorously among themselves about current policies and programmes, ends and methods, much as they do with other men. If they did not, we would have a new dogmatism to contend with. Rather we must allow for a diversity in Humanist convictions and Humanists should be willing to tolerate pluralistic political positions. Humanism cannot be expected to provide a specific economic or political theory, or a specific social or technological solution to every problem. Nor should it be expected to offer a total world view which will answer all the questions that people raise, or offer itself as the salvation of mankind. Humanists in the last analysis should be sceptical, and especially of their own pretensions. They are well aware that religions have promised salvation in the past and have failed, as have modern ideological guarantees of utopia. Alas, life is too complex to lend itself to easy solutions. And new problems appear as quickly as we solve old ones. A mature Humanist wisdom, accordingly, would allow many flowers to bloom, many paths to be taken, many alternative styles of life. Thus Humanism must be pluralistic about concrete issues.

Is there anything that all Humanists share? Assuredly, as I have pointed out, a set of moral ideals which are committed to saving and enhancing the qualities of human experience, but primarily a commitment to the use of critical intelligence. And this means that where critical intelligence enters, Humanist tactics or programmes will vary in relationship to the social context and solutions. Most Humanists emphasize the use of toleration, dialogue and negotiation as the chief methods for solving human problems. In principle, the Humanist abhors the easy resort to violence. Yet he is not an absolutist. For the use of violence depends upon the particular context at hand. Sometimes the Humanist will feel it necessary, on the basis of the evidence, to call for revolution and for the violent destruction of a corrupt society—if there are no other means available for social change or compromise. Moreover, he may be willing to use violence on the international level, as in the war against fascism, pending the development of a genuine world order. At other times Humanists will feel convinced that certain essential values have to be preserved; though he may be called a conservative, he finds that he must stand against those who proclaim a new order and who are impervious to the claims of freedom of speech, free thought or the rights of man.

The Humanist should not be fearful of being labelled: that is a trap for the timid. One can, I submit, be a liberal Humanist, a Marxist Humanist, a radical Humanist, a conservative Humanist, even a reactionary Humanist—if the times demand. It all depends upon the context and the alternatives before us.

The development of civilization is a slow and uphill battle in which intelligence—fused with compassion—comes to prevail. It is a long struggle in which blind sentiment and unreasoned custom are questioned and transformed by reason. Humanism, in the last analysis, has as its chief commitment, a commitment to the ethic of

183

the free mind. For the freethinker in religion, politics, morality, art and science the only authority is the authority of intelligence, the only master is reason. If a man uses his moral ideals as guidelines, always modifying them by his intelligence, and if he cherishes and respects morally the dignity, worth and fulfilment of human beings, then he is a Humanist—whether he is a liberal, radical or conservative. Humanists of different political persuasions can still share common moral values. At least that is the view that I wish to propose at a moment in history when liberalism and conservatism are being transformed, and political allegiances and alliances questioned and altered. The basic worship of the Humanist is the worship of the free mind; and his highest duty is to the truth as he sees it and to the destruction of cant, fraud, deception, illusion or dogma. That is why I would exclude Pope Paul VI from the range of Humanism, because for him faith has become a substitute for reason and piety, for dependence upon human resources. And I would question the use of the term Humanism by orthodox Marxist-Leninists who, although they share with Humanists the rejection of supernaturalism and a wish to build a better world, nevertheless are willing to compromise their means to achieve their ends and to sacrifice the freedom of the individual and suppress civil liberties, including intellectual and artistic liberty—as the victimization of Alexander Solzhenitsyn so vividly demonstrates. This indictment would not refer to Marxists who are thoroughgoing democratic socialists and who share Humanist methods and ends. It would apply, I am sorry to say, to many so-called 'radical' youth in the West who have been captured by a new passionate religiosity and have often, in the process, abandoned the use of critical intelligence or the use of open and more democratic methods in solving social problems.

Humanism, in this sense, is always the most radical of moral positions, for it involves an uncompromising and basic commitment to the use of evidence in all areas of life. I like to use the term 'critical radicalism', for it is a radicalism informed by intelligence. But I am talking about independence and heresy in thought; thus it is liberal in the sense that it is willing and able to examine all sides of a question, to innovate and explore and, if need be, adapt new departures in belief and action. In one sense, this is also the proper meaning of liberalism at its best: liberalism as a method of inquiry, according to John Dewey, rather than a specific programme

184

of action. If one is willing to accept this definition of liberalism, then liberalism and Humanism are very close. But many liberals today wish to identify liberalism solely with a specific platform or programme of social reform. If one insists upon this definition of liberalism, then liberalism and Humanism are not necessarily the same, though they need not be antithetical.

But Humanism may also be labelled conservative in some contexts—such as in the universities today—where it is committed to the defence of academic freedom against those who are willing to sacrifice it at the altar of moral and ideological purism.

Thus the Humanist ideal is neither liberal nor radical nor conservative, but can be any or all, depending upon the demands of the situation. For as I have said, if Humanism in the final analysis is dedicated to respect for the principle of free inquiry, then we must follow the dictates of that inquiry wherever it may lead.

This definition of Humanism, which relates Humanism to free thought, does not exclude other important moral principles of Humanism, as spelled out above. Emphasizing the centrality of free thought as a Humanist ideal, however, accords in some sense with ordinary usage. It permits us to classify certain individuals or groups as humanistic and to exclude others, without debasing the term entirely. And at the same time it is a proposal, governing how we shall use the term in the future. The co-option of the term Humanism by orthodox Catholics or totalitarian Marxists, who do not recognize the demands of freedom of thought about fundamental religious or ideological questions, is an untenable contradiction of what is essential to Humanism.

We should, of course, applaud the humanization and liberalization of Catholicism and Marxism, and Humanists should welcome continued dialogue with liberal Catholics and Marxist Humanists. But it is a gross distortion to characterize those orthodox doctrines as humanistic which deny the fundamental commitment to the ideals of free thought. There are other important Humanist principles besides free thought and we do judge doctrines by the degree to which they believe in the fulfilment of human potentialities, have some confidence in human powers, are opposed to the dehumanization of man, and are concerned with the whole of humanity, and so on. But surely we should insist that a theistic religion or totalitarian ideology cannot be considered humanistic in its essential

185

nature if one of the most basic of human rights—the right of individuals to the free use of knowledge—is ignored.

This is the constant message of Humanism, in the classical Hellenistic period, in the Renaissance, during the Enlightenment and in the twentieth century. And it is a message that Humanism should never be willing to compromise. For it is in essence the heart of the Humanist ideal.

NOTES ON CONTRIBUTORS

KHOREN ARISIAN, associate editor of *The Humanist* in America, is an ethical leader of the New York Society for Ethical Culture.

ALGERNON D. BLACK is a senior ethical leader of the New York Society for Ethical Culture. He is author of *The People and the Police*.

H. J. BLACKHAM, former director of the British Humanist Association, is author of *Humanism, Objections to Humanism* and *Religion in a Modern Society* among other works.

JOSEPH BLAU is Professor of Religion at Columbia University, where he was also chairman. He is the author of *Men and Movements in American Philosophy* and *Modern Varieties of Judaism*, and has edited *Cornerstones of Religious Freedom in America*.

MIRIAM ALLEN deFORD is a distinguished essayist, biographer, novelist, journalist, historian and poet. Among other books, she has written *Up-Hill All the Way*, a biography of her husband, Maynard Shipley, who was one of the signers of the Humanist Manifesto. Miss deFord reviews crime for the *San Francisco Chronicle*.

RAYA DUNAYEVSKAYA, noted Marxist scholar and former secretary to Leon Trotsky, is the author of *Marxism and Freedom* and other works.

EDWARD L. ERICSON is a former president of the American Ethical Union and leader of the New York Society for Ethical Culture.

H. J. EYSENCK is Professor of Psychology at the London University Institute of Psychiatry. Among his books are *Sense and Nonsense in*

Psychology and *The Biological Basis of Personality*; he is also chief editor of *Behaviour Research and Therapy*. Professor Eysenck is a board member of the British Humanist Association.

ROY P. FAIRFIELD is a Professor of Political Science at Antioch College and director of the Union for Experimental Colleges. An associate editor of *The Humanist*, he has edited the book *Humanistic Frontiers in American Education*.

HORACE L. FRIESS was formerly Professor of Philosophy and Religion at Columbia University, and Chairman of the Department of Religion. A former editor of *The Journal of Religion*, he has served on the board of directors of the American Ethical Union.

GORA is founder and head of the Atheistic Center in Vijayawada, India, and editor of the journal *The Atheist*.

SIDNEY HOOK is Professor of Philosophy at New York University. A former student of John Dewey, Professor Hook is author of *The Quest for Being*, *The Metaphysics of Pragmatism*, *Reason, Social Myths and Democracy* and *Political Power and Personal Freedom*. He is president of University Centers for Rational Alternatives and former president of the American Philosophical Association. A frequent contributor to *The Humanist*, he was for many years on its editorial board.

LESTER A. KIRKENDALL, a member of the publications committee of *The Humanist*, was a Professor of Family Life at Oregon State University from 1949 to 1969. Recently he has lectured widely on interpersonal relationships and sexual education. He is author of *Premarital Intercourse and Interpersonal Relationships*, and has co-edited *The New Sexual Revolution*.

PAUL KURTZ is Professor of Philosophy at the State University of New York at Buffalo and editor of *The Humanist* in America. He is a member of the board of directors of the American Humanist Association and of the International Humanist and Ethical Union. He is author of *Decision and the Condition of Man*, and co-author of *A Current Appraisal of the Behavioural Sciences*. He also edited *Moral Problems in Contemporary Society: Essays in Humanistic Ethics*, *Tolerance and Revolution* (with S. Stojanović), and *A Catholic/Humanist Dialogue* (with A. Dondeyne).

188

CORLISS LAMONT is author of *Philosophy of Humanism, A Humanist Wedding Service, The Illusion of Immortality* and other books. He is the first recipient of the 'John Dewey Humanist Award'.

KENNETH MACCORQUODALE is Professor of Philosophy at the University of Minnesota. He is co-author of *Modern Learning Theory* and editor of the Century Psychology Series.

FLOYD MATSON is Professor of American Studies at the University of Hawaii, Honolulu. He is former president of the American Association for Humanistic Psychology and author of *The Broken Image* and *Being, Becoming and Behaviour*.

LLOYD MORAIN and MARY MORAIN are co-authors of the book *Humanism as the Next Step,* and are on the Editorial Board of *The Humanist*.

MATHILDE NIEL is associated with L'Institute de L'Homme in Paris. She is author of numerous works and has contributed to Erich Fromm's book *Socialist Humanism*. She also participated in the Marxist-non-Marxist Humanist Dialogue in Yugoslavia.

BERNARD PHILLIPS, Professor of Religion at Temple University, Philadelphia, has spent much time in Zen monasteries and has edited the writing of D. T. Suzuki.

JOHN HERMAN RANDALL Jr. is F. J. E. Woodbridge Professor Emeritus of Philosophy at Columbia University. A former editor of the *Journal of Philosophy*, he is author of *Career of Philosophy* and *The Meaning of Religion for Man*, among other books.

HERBERT W. SCHNEIDER is Professor of Philosophy and Dean at Claremont Graduate School in California. He is an editor of *The Journal of the History of Philosophy* and for many years was editor of *The Journal of Philosophy*. He is the author of many books, including *History of American Philosophy*, *Religion in Twentieth Century America*, *The Puritan in America* and *Morals for Mankind*. He is a member of both the American Humanist Association and the American Ethical Union.

189

ROY WOOD SELLARS, Professor Emeritus at the University of Michigan, is a distinguished American philosopher and author of the original *A Humanist Manifesto* of 1933.

B. F. SKINNER is considered to be the leading behaviourist psychologist in the world. He is author of *Walden II*, among other works.

DAVID TRIBE, president of the Secular Society of Great Britain, is the author of *100 Years of Free Thought*.

J. P. VAN PRAAG is president of the International Humanist and Ethical Union. He serves in the Dutch Government and is Professor of Philosophy at Utrecht.

GARDNER WILLIAMS was Professor of Philosophy at Toledo University in Toledo, Ohio. He was president of the Toledo Humanist Chapter, and author of the book *Humanistic Ethics*.

EDWIN WILSON is former editor of *The Humanist* in America and of *Religious Humanism*. A past director of the American Humanist Association, he was also founder of the Fellowship of Religious Humanists.

MARVIN ZIMMERMAN is Associate Professor of Philosophy at the State University of New York at Buffalo. He is author of the book *Contemporary Problems of Democracy*. He was formerly chairman of the New York City chapter of the American Humanist Association.

190